my first
Hands-On
BiBLe

Preschoolers
experience the fun!
Live the Truth!

Tyndale House Publishers, Inc.
Carol Stream, Illinois

Visit Tyndale's website for kids at www.tyndale.com/kids.

Visit Group's exciting websites at www.4everybuddy.com and www.Group.com.

TYNDALE, New Living Translation, NLT, the New Living Translation logo, and LeatherLike are registered trademarks of Tyndale House Publishers, Inc. The Tyndale Kids logo is a trademark of Tyndale House Publishers, Inc.

Hands-On Bible, Hands-On Bible Curriculum, and the Group logo are registered trademarks of Group Publishing, Inc. The Hands-On Bible logo and the Hands-On Bible Curriculum logo are trademarks of Group Publishing, Inc.

My First Hands-On Bible

Editorial Team: Sue Geiman, Erin Gwynne, Becki Manni, Joani Schultz, Betty Free Swanberg, Ali Thompson, Stephanie Voiland, and Christine Yount Jones

Design Team: Jean Bruns, Daniel Farrell, and Randy Maid

Illustrators: Paige Billin-Frye and Jane Yamada, represented by Portfolio Solutions, LLC

Writers: Renée Gray-Wilburn, Marsha Maxfield Hall, Jan Kershner, Janna Kinner, Julie Lavender, Barbie Murphy, Karen Pennington, Janet R. Reeves, Elaine Ernst Schneider, Donna K. Simcoe, Courtney Walsh, and Dana Wilkerson

Scripture quotations are taken from the Holy Bible, New Living Translation, copyright © 1996, 2004, 2007 by Tyndale House Foundation. Used by permission of Tyndale House Publishers, Inc., Carol Stream, Illinois 60188. All rights reserved.

For manufacturing information regarding this product, please call 1-800-323-9400.

Library of Congress Cataloging-in-Publication Data

Bible. English. New Living Translation. Selections. 2011.
  My first hands-on Bible / [writers, Renée Gray-Wilburn et al.].
     p. cm.
  ISBN 978-1-4143-4830-8 (hc)
  I. Gray-Wilburn, Renée. II. Title.
  BS391.3.G73 2011
  220.9'505—dc22   2011005493

ISBN 978-1-4964-0643-9 sc
ISBN 978-1-4964-0644-6 Bold Blue LeatherLike
ISBN 978-1-4964-0645-3 Pretty Pink LeatherLike

Printed in China

21 20 19 18 17 16 15
12 11 10 9 8 7 6

Contents

New Testament

How to Use My First Hands-On Bible

Welcome to *My First Hands-On Bible*! You and your child will explore God's Word together in fun and exciting ways as you read this Bible. You'll get to dig in to the Bible passages with fun activities as you read them, and then follow up your reading with simple activities that will make the Bible a part of your child's life.

Real Bible Text

My First Hands-On Bible is special because it's the only preschool Bible with actual Bible text! We selected the New Living Translation (NLT) for its clarity for readers of all ages. Hearing Scripture in its true form will be a powerful experience for your child. 2 Timothy 3:16 tells us, "All Scripture is inspired by God and is useful to teach us what is true and to make us realize what is wrong in our lives." With this Bible, your child can hear the God-inspired words of his book, the Bible.

We abridged the NLT passages to provide the most age-appropriate Scripture for preschoolers. You may find, though, that you occasionally come across a word that's unfamiliar to your child. If that's the case, stop and help your child understand what's happening in the part of the Bible you're reading. Or after you read a passage, ask your child to tell you what happened in the Bible story, and fill in any gaps in your own words.

Hands-On Activities

As you read, you'll come across colored handprints in the Bible text. When you see a handprint, stop reading, and lead your child in the activity by the matching handprint. These are written for you to read aloud to your children. You'll get your child involved in the Bible passage through moving around, acting out, looking for things in the pictures, and enjoying all sorts of other fun, hands-on activities. The Bible will come alive for your child through these hands-on activities!

(Note: The handprints are there to help your child experience the story as he or she hears it. It may be helpful for some children to stop and do each activity at the spot indicated in the Bible passage, while other children may benefit from reading the story all the way through and then going back to do the activities later.)

Time to Pray and Let's Talk

Each passage ends with a prayer that makes the point of the Scripture personal. Discussion questions help you and your child discover how the Bible connects to your lives. Pray these prayers and discuss these questions with your child to help make your Bible reading meaningful. These are great ways for you and your child to interact with each other as you explore the meaning of the Scripture you've just read together.

Pockets and Cuddles

Your child will love how these adorable animals guide you both in making discoveries. Your child can easily find the prayer by looking for Pockets, the kangaroo. Likewise, Cuddles, the lamb, leads you and your child in the activities with each Bible story.

These fun characters give your child something familiar with each Bible story. Your child will look for Pockets and Cuddles in anticipation of fun learning.

To bring these recurring characters to your home, you can find Pockets and Cuddles puppets for sale at http://store.grouppublishing.com.

Activities

Each Bible story has two activities with it. These are simple activities, and many of them are things you can do as you go through your normal routines. These activities make it easy for you to make the Scripture a part of your child's life. They're a great way to review the story with your child the next day or later that week.

Read these on your own, and plan a time to lead your child through them. You may choose to do both of the activities or just one. Either way, each activity reinforces the Scripture to your child.

Jesus Connection

Each passage ends with a "Jesus Connection." Your child will see that Jesus is the center of all Scripture, even passages that don't mention him. And your child will know that Jesus is a real part of life. So read these Jesus Connections to your child as a great way to show Jesus' presence in all of Scripture.

THE
Jesus
CONNECTION

Thank you for choosing *My First Hands-On Bible* for your child. God will use you to bring the Bible to life as you and your child go through it together!

God Creates

Genesis 1

In the beginning God created the heavens and the earth. ²The earth was formless and empty, and darkness covered the deep waters. And the Spirit of God was hovering over the surface of the waters.

³Then God said, "Let there be light," and there was light.⁴ And God saw that the light was good. Then he separated the light from the darkness.

⁶Then God said, "Let there be a space

"Cover your eyes for a few seconds and imagine what the earth was like."

the World

between the waters, to separate the waters
of the heavens from the waters of the earth."

⁹Then God said, "Let the waters beneath the
sky flow together into one place, so dry ground
may appear." And that is what happened.

"Turn a light off and on as you say, 'Let there be light!'"

11

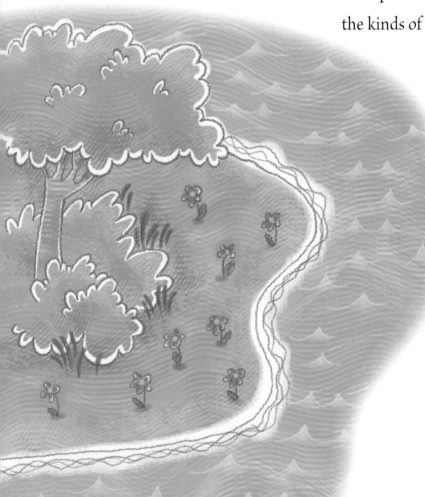

"Squat down like you're a little seed, then stand up like a tall tree."

¹⁰God called the dry ground "land" and the waters "seas." And God saw that it was good. ¹¹Then God said, "Let the land sprout with vegetation—every sort of seed-bearing plant, and trees that grow seed-bearing fruit. These seeds will then produce the kinds of

"Make a fish face."

plants and trees

from which they came."

And that is what happened.

[16]God made two great lights—the larger

one to govern the day, and the smaller one to

govern the night. He also made the stars.

[20]Then God said, "Let the waters swarm

with fish and other life. Let the skies

be filled with birds of every kind." [21]So God

created great sea creatures and every living

thing that scurries and swarms in the water,

and every sort of bird—each producing

"Let's draw a
sun and a moon.
Then let's sing
'Twinkle, Twinkle
Little Star.'"

offspring of the same kind. And God saw that it was good.

²⁵God made all sorts of wild animals, livestock, and small animals, each able to produce offspring of the same kind. And God saw that it was good.

"Act like your favorite animal."

THE
Jesus
CONNECTION The Bible tells us

Let's Talk

- What's your favorite thing that God made?
- If you could change one thing that God made, what would it be?

Dear God, thank you for making such an amazing world for us. We love it—and we love you! In Jesus' name, amen.

Pockets says, *"It's time to pray!"*

Cloud Watching

Look at the sky this week to see if any clouds look like animal shapes to you. God made all those clouds—*and* every animal you can think of.

A New Creation

With your child, draw pretend animals. Then talk about the animals you made and the animals God made.

Cuddles says, *"Let's get creative!"*

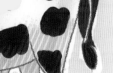

God created everything with his Son, Jesus.

Then God said, "Let us make human beings in our image, to be like us. 👋 They will reign over the fish in the sea, the birds in the sky, the livestock, all the wild animals on the earth, and the small animals that scurry along the ground."

²⁷ So God created human beings in his own image. In the image of God he created them;

"Look in a mirror at your image. God made us in his image!"

Creates People

Genesis 1-2

male and female he created them.

²⁸Then God blessed them and said, "Be fruitful and multiply. Fill the earth and govern it. Reign over the fish in the sea, the birds in the sky, and all the animals that scurry along the ground."

¹⁸Then the LORD God said, "It is not good

"Pretend to swim like a fish, fly like a bird, and walk like an animal."

"If you had to call lions by a different name, what would it be? How about elephants?"

for the man to be alone. I will make a helper who is just right for him." ¹⁹So the LORD God formed from the ground all the wild animals and all the birds of the sky. He brought them to the man to see what he would call them, and the man chose a name for each one. ²⁰He gave names to all the livestock, all the birds of the sky, and all the wild animals. But still there was no helper just right for him.

18

²¹So the LORD God caused the man to fall into a deep sleep. While the man slept, the LORD God took out one of the man's ribs and closed up the opening. ²²Then the LORD God made a woman from the rib, and he brought her to the man.

²³"At last!" the man exclaimed.

"This one is bone from my bone, and flesh

"Make some snoring sounds!"

"Can you feel your ribs? How many can you count?"

19

from my flesh! She will be called 'woman,' because she was taken from 'man.'"

[24]This explains why a man leaves his father and mother and is joined to his wife, and the two are united into one.

THE Jesus CONNECTION

God made us in his image, but we are not exactly like God. Only Jesus is just like God!

Rhyme Time

Say this fun rhyme together, and do the motions
in parentheses.

God made people, *(pound fists on top of each other)*
Both short and tall. *(crouch low, then stand up tall)*
God made people, *(pound fists on top of each other)*
He made them all! *(point outward and turn in a circle)*

Cuddles says,
"Let's rhyme!"

People Plans

Make a person shape out of modeling
dough. Talk about how God makes each
person in your family special.

Pockets says,
"It's time to pray!"

Let's Talk

• How can we take care of God's earth?
• What did God make special about you?

Dear God, you're
amazing! Thank you
for making us in your
image so we are like you.
In Jesus' name, amen.

"Pretend you're
a snake. Can you
move around
without using your
arms or legs?"

The serpent
was the shrewdest of
all the wild animals the LORD God
had made. One day he asked the woman,
"Did God really say you must not eat the fruit
from any of the trees in the garden?"

"How many
different kinds of
fruit can you find
on this page?"

²"Of course we may eat fruit from the trees
in the garden," the woman replied. ³"It's only the
fruit from the tree in the middle of the garden
that we are not allowed to eat. God said, 'You

Eve's Sin

must not eat it or even touch it; if you do, you will die.'"

⁴"You won't die!" the serpent replied to the woman. ⁵"God knows that your eyes will be opened as soon as you eat it, and you will be like God, knowing both good and evil."

"Close your eyes, and then open them really big."

⁶The woman was convinced. She saw that the tree was beautiful and its fruit looked delicious, and she wanted the wisdom it would give her. So she took some of the fruit and ate it.

Then she gave some to her husband, who was with her, and he ate it, too. ⁷At that moment their eyes were opened, and they suddenly felt shame at their nakedness. So they sewed fig leaves together to cover themselves.

Pockets says, "It's time to pray!"

Dear God, please help us to make good choices and do what's right when we have to choose between good and bad. In Jesus' name, amen.

Let's Talk

- What are some rules you have to follow?
- What happens when you don't obey the rules?
- What are some things you can do to obey God's rules?

THE Jesus CONNECTION

Plant Safari

Look for different kinds of plants with your child, including fruits, vegetables, and decorative plants. Help your child determine whether or not the plant can be eaten. Talk about how God's rules keep us safe.

Cuddles says, "Let's find plants!"

House Rules

With your child, make a list of some of the rules in your house. At the end of the week, talk about which rules were hardest for your child to follow and why those rules are important.

Like Adam and Eve, we sometimes sin and feel bad. The good news is that Jesus will always forgive us!

Noah

When Noah was 600 years old, on the seventeenth day of the second month, all the underground waters erupted from the earth, and the rain fell in mighty torrents from the sky. [12]The rain continued to fall for forty days and forty nights.

[13]That very day Noah had gone into the boat with his wife and his sons—Shem, Ham, and Japheth—and their wives. [14]With them in the boat were pairs of every kind of animal—domestic and wild, large and small—along

"Make rain sounds with me! First we'll rub our hands together, then clap them quietly, then clap them loudly, and then pat our hands on our legs."

and the Flood

Genesis 7:11-20

with birds of every kind. ¹⁵Two by two they came into the boat, representing every living thing that breathes.  ¹⁶A male and female of each kind entered, just as God had commanded Noah. Then the LORD closed the door behind them.

¹⁷For forty days the

"Walk like an elephant, hop like a kangaroo, and run like a deer."

"What animals can you find on this page? What do they say?"

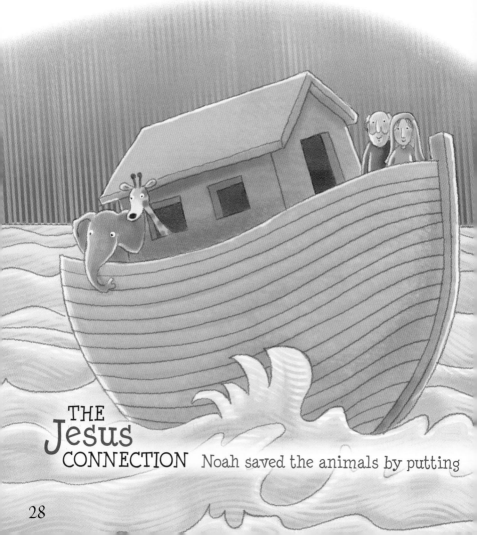

"Pretend you're in the big floating boat, sometimes called an ark, rocking back and forth."

floodwaters grew deeper, covering the ground and lifting the boat high above the earth. [18] As the waters rose higher and higher above the ground, the boat floated safely on the surface. [19] Finally, the water covered even the highest mountains on the earth, [20] rising more than twenty-two feet above the highest peaks.

THE Jesus CONNECTION Noah saved the animals by putting

Pockets says, "It's time to pray!"

Dear God, we know you can help us do hard things like Noah did. Help us to trust you when hard things happen. In Jesus' name, amen.

Let's Talk

- What's something that's hard for you to do?
- How could God help you?

Safari

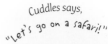

Cuddles says, "Let's go on a safari!"

This week, look for animals with your child, and talk about all the animals God kept safe on Noah's ark. Think of times when your family can trust God to keep you safe.

Tub Time

Give your child a plastic bowl to float in the tub as an ark. If you have small, waterproof animal toys, put them in the boat. Have your child make animal sounds and float the ark. Talk about how Noah trusted God in the ark and how we can trust God.

them on the ark. And God sent someone to save us—Jesus!

29

God's Rainbow Promise

Genesis 8-9

"Blow like the wind."

But God remembered Noah and all the wild animals and livestock with him in the boat. He sent a wind to blow across the earth, and the floodwaters began to recede.

[8] Then God told Noah and his sons, [9] "I hereby confirm my covenant with you and your descendants, [10] and with all the animals that were

"What colors do you see in the picture of a rainbow?"

on the boat with you—the birds, the livestock, and all the wild animals—every living creature on earth. [11]Yes, I am confirming my covenant with you. Never again will floodwaters kill all living creatures; never again will a flood destroy the earth."

[12]Then God said, "I am giving you a sign of my covenant with you and with all living creatures, for all generations to come. [13]I have placed my rainbow in the clouds. It is the sign of my covenant with you and with all the earth. [14]When I send clouds over the earth, the rainbow will appear in the clouds, [15]and I will remember my covenant with

"Make a rainbow by putting your fingers together."

31

"Blow on your rainbow to remind us that God keeps his promise even when it's stormy and the wind blows."

you and with all living creatures. Never again will the floodwaters destroy all life. ¹⁶When I see the rainbow in the clouds, I will remember the eternal covenant between God and every living creature on earth." ¹⁷Then God said to Noah, "Yes, this rainbow is the sign of the covenant I am confirming with all the creatures on earth."

"Hold your arms up high with your fingers together, and thank God for his rainbow promise."

THE Jesus CONNECTION Here's another promise

Shopping Search

Cuddles says, "Let's go shopping!"

While grocery shopping, have your child look for different colors on packaging. Whenever you check out, remind your child of the colors you saw and say, "God keeps his promises to all living creatures."

Rainbow Light

Hold a DVD shiny side up under a lamp, flashlight, or sunny window. Slowly move the DVD around to see the rainbow and identify its colors. Or create your own "rain" and rainbow outdoors with a fine spray from a hose. Talk about the promise God made and keeps today.

Let's Talk

- What's a promise you've made?
- Tell about a time someone kept a promise to you.

Pockets says, "It's time to pray!"

Dear God, thank you for making promises and keeping them. Thank you that you promise to always be with us. In Jesus' name, amen.

God made: He forgives us because Jesus died for our sins.

The Tower of Babel

Genesis 11:1-9

At one time all the people of the world spoke the same language and used the same words. ²As the people migrated to the east, they found a plain in the land of Babylonia and settled there.

³They began saying to each other, "Let's make

"Pretend to make
some bricks! First
pretend to scoop
some clay and
shape it. Then pat
the bricks and
stack them."

bricks and harden them
with fire." (In this region
bricks were used instead of
stone, and tar was used for
mortar.) ⁴Then they said,
"Come, let's build a great city for
ourselves with a tower that reaches
into the sky. This will make us famous
and keep us from being scattered all over
the world."

⁵But the LORD came down to look at the
city and the tower the people
were building. ⁶"Look!"
he said. "The

"Reach as high
as you can!"

"Count to three
in Spanish! Uno,
dos, tres."

people are united, and
they all speak the same
language. After this, nothing
they set out to do will
be impossible for them!
⁷Come, let's go down
and confuse the people
with different languages.
Then they won't be able to
understand each other."

⁸In that way, the LORD
scattered them all over the world, and they
stopped building the city. ⁹That is why the
city was called Babel, because that is where
the LORD confused the people with different
languages. In this way he scattered them all
over the world.

"Pretend you're
people who are
scattering to
places all over
the world! Run
to whatever place
I point to."

THE
Jesus CONNECTION   The people in the Bible

Pockets says, "It's time to pray!"

Dear God, sometimes we think we can do whatever we want without your help. Please teach us to ask for your help to do what pleases you.

In Jesus' name, amen.

Tower Power

Have your child try to build a block tower up to the ceiling without any help. As he or she builds the tower that eventually falls or can't be completed, discuss how the people in the Bible were proud and thought they didn't need God's help. Talk about why it's important to ask God to help us.

Cuddles says, "Let's eat new food!"

Foreign Foods

For one meal this week, have your family's favorite ethnic food. Talk about ways your country is different from other countries. Pray that people from different countries will learn that God loves them.

Let's Talk

• What do you like to do all by yourself?
• What can God help you with this week?

couldn't get to God by building a tall tower. But we can be close to God by trusting Jesus to forgive our sins.

God's Promise

Genesis 15, 17

Then the LORD took Abram outside and said to him, "Look up into the sky and count the stars if you can. That's how many descendants you will have!"

"Count as many stars as you can on this page."

[1]When Abram was ninety-nine years old, the LORD appeared to him and said, "I am El-Shaddai—'God Almighty.' Serve me faithfully and live a blameless life. [2]I will make a covenant with you, by which I will guarantee to give you countless descendants."

to Abraham

"Lay with your
face down like
Abram did."

³At this, Abram fell face down on the
ground. 👋 Then God said to him, ⁴"This is
my covenant with you: I will make you the
father of a multitude of nations! ⁵What's more,
I am changing your name. It will no longer be
Abram. Instead, you will be called Abraham,
for you will be the father of many nations. 👋

"Say your
full name."

"God promised to love Abraham's family and to make it a big family. Name some people you know who love God. They all belong to Abraham's family!"

⁶"I will make you extremely fruitful. Your descendants will become many nations, and kings will be among them!

⁷"I will confirm my covenant with you and your descendants after you, from generation to generation. This is the everlasting covenant: I will always be your God and the God of your descendants after you."

Pockets says, "It's time to pray!"

Dear God, thank you for keeping your promise to love Abraham and his family. Help us to love you and trust you, just like Abraham did. In Jesus' name, amen.

Let's Talk

- What do people do to show they love you?
- What does God do to show he loves you?

THE
Jesus CONNECTION

Promise Cheer

Repeat this cheer with your child while you're driving or walking somewhere this week:

**Promises, promises,
God keeps his promises!
God keeps his promise
to love me
(help me,
forgive me,
teach me)!**

Cuddles says,
"Let's cheer!"

Uncountable Stars

On a clear night, take your family outside, and have your child try to count as many stars as possible. Talk about how God promised Abraham as many grandkids as there are stars—and that he promised to love them.

God kept his promise to Abraham. And God will keep his promise to us that we can go to heaven if we believe in Jesus.

"Grab a doll or stuffed animal and hold it like you would hold a baby."

The LORD kept his word and did for Sarah exactly what he had promised. ²She became pregnant, and she gave birth to a son for Abraham in his old age. This happened at just the time God had said it would.

Is Born

Genesis 21:1-7

³And Abraham named their son Isaac. ⁴Eight
days after Isaac was born, Abraham
circumcised him as God had commanded.
⁵Abraham was 100 years old
when Isaac was born.

⁶And Sarah
declared, "God
has brought
me laughter.
All who hear
about this
will laugh
with me.

"Clap your hands
100 times."

⁷Who would have said to Abraham that Sarah would nurse a baby? Yet I have given Abraham a son in his old age!"

"Sarah laughed because she was happy. Let out a really happy laugh."

THE Jesus CONNECTION God gave us the best gift when he

Pockets says, "it's time to pray!"

Dear God, you gave Sarah a baby, and that made her very happy. Help us to be happy and say thank you when you give us good gifts. In Jesus' name, amen.

Let's Talk

• What are some of the best things God has given you?
• What are some things you want God to give you?

Beautiful Babies

Cuddles says, "let's find babies!"

Look for babies this week. Whenever your child sees a baby, talk with your child about God's gift to Sarah. And talk about things God has given you.

Gifts from God

With your child, collect several things around the house that are gifts from God. Talk about how each thing is a gift from God, and thank him for each gift you've collected.

gave us Jesus, who loves us, helps us, and forgives us.

Jacob

"Touch something furry to see what Baby Esau felt like."

And when the time came to give birth, Rebekah discovered that she did indeed have twins! [25]The first one was very red at birth and covered with thick hair like a fur coat. So they named him Esau. [26]Then the other twin was born with his hand grasping Esau's

46

Tricks Esau

Genesis 25:24-34

heel. So they named him Jacob.  Isaac was sixty years old when the twins were born.

²⁷ As the boys grew up, Esau became a skillful hunter. He was an outdoorsman,

"Grab your heel."

"Pretend to do your favorite outside activity. Now pretend to do your favorite inside activity."

but Jacob had a quiet temperament, preferring to stay at home. ²⁸ Isaac loved Esau because he enjoyed eating the wild game Esau brought home, but Rebekah loved Jacob.

²⁹ One day when Jacob was cooking some stew, Esau arrived home from the wilderness exhausted and hungry. ³⁰ Esau said to Jacob, "I'm starved! Give me some of that red

stew!" (This is how Esau got his other name, Edom, which means "red.")

³¹"All right," Jacob replied, "but trade me your rights as the firstborn son."

³²"Look, I'm dying of starvation!" said Esau. "What good is my birthright to me now?"

³³But Jacob said, "First you must swear that your birthright is mine." So Esau swore an oath, thereby selling all his rights as the firstborn to his brother, Jacob.

"Show what you look like when you're hungry and tired."

49

[34]Then Jacob gave Esau some bread and lentil stew. Esau ate the meal, then got up and left. He showed contempt for his rights as the firstborn.

THE Jesus CONNECTION

Jacob's trade with Esau was greedy. But Jesus made a good trade for you—he traded his life so you could live forever with him.

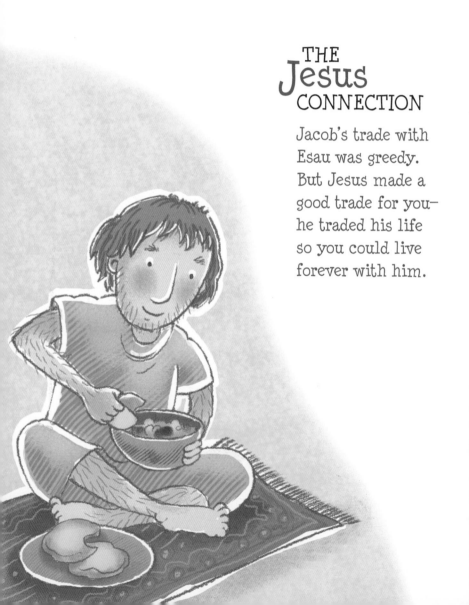

Supper Time

Make stew or soup for supper one night this week. With careful supervision, let your child help you add ingredients to the pot. Thank God for providing food and other things your family needs.

Cuddles says, "Let's make stew!"

Want to Trade?

Get out a crumpled piece of paper and your child's favorite toy. Give your child the piece of paper while you hold the toy. Ask your child which one is better, then ask if he or she wants to trade. Explain that Jacob and Esau's trade was like that—one thing was much better than the other! The oldest son got a lot of power and special things, and that was way better than a bowl of stew!

Pockets says, "It's time to pray!"

Let's Talk

- What do you do when you want something you don't have?
- What does God want you to do when you need something?

Dear God, help me not to trick people the way Jacob did. And make me wise about using the good gifts you've given me, not foolish like Esau was. In Jesus' name, amen.

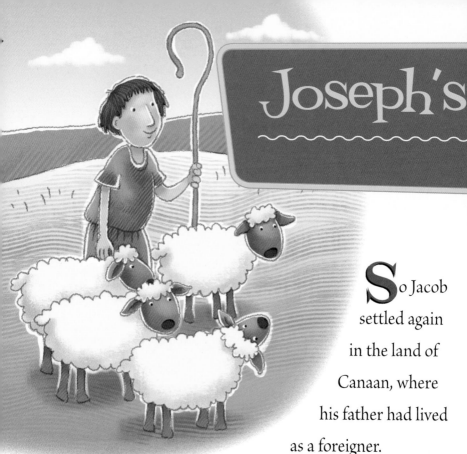

Joseph's

So Jacob settled again in the land of Canaan, where his father had lived as a foreigner.

² This is the account of Jacob and his family. When Joseph was seventeen years old, he often tended his father's flocks. He worked for his half brothers, the sons of his father's wives Bilhah and Zilpah. But Joseph reported to his father some of the bad things his brothers were doing.

³ Jacob loved Joseph more than any of his other children because Joseph had been born

"Pretend you're a shepherd. Take out a stuffed animal, and gently guide it across the room."

Colorful Coat

Genesis 37:1-4

"Shake your finger back and forth."

"What colors do you see in Joseph's coat? Which is your favorite color?"

to him in his old age. So one day Jacob had a special gift made for Joseph—a beautiful robe.  ⁴ But his brothers hated Joseph because their father loved him more than the rest of them. They couldn't say a kind word to him.

THE Jesus CONNECTION Jacob loved Joseph and gave him a

54

Pockets says, "It's time to pray!"

Lord, you have given us so many wonderful things. Please help us to be happy when other people get gifts too. In Jesus' name, amen.

Let's Talk

• What are some gifts people have given you?
• What gifts have people given your sister (brother, friends)?

Dress Up

Cuddles says, "Let's wear coats!"

Have your child try on each coat your family owns. Talk about the colors on each coat. Thank God for giving your family clothes to wear.

Colorful Necklace

Show your child how to use markers or paint to color uncooked macaroni and string it into a necklace. Have your child give the necklace to someone. Help your child tell the person about Joseph's gift in the Bible.

coat. God loves us and sent us a special gift—Jesus.

Joseph's Brothers Get Mean

Genesis 37:23-36

So when Joseph arrived, his brothers ripped off the beautiful robe he was wearing. ²⁴Then they grabbed him and threw him into the cistern. Now the cistern was empty; there was no water in it. ²⁵Then, just as they were sitting down to eat, they looked up and saw a caravan of

"Count Joseph's older brothers in this picture."

56

camels in the distance coming toward them. It was a group of Ishmaelite traders taking a load of gum, balm, and aromatic resin from Gilead down to Egypt.

²⁶Judah said to his brothers, ²⁷"Instead of hurting him, let's sell him to those Ishmaelite traders. After all, he is our brother—our own flesh and blood!" And his brothers agreed. ²⁸So when the Ishmaelites, who were Midianite traders, came by, Joseph's brothers pulled him out of the cistern and sold him

"Pretend you're on a camel, and ride across the room like the traders."

57

"Pretend you're in a deep hole and need help getting out."

to them for twenty pieces of silver. And the traders took him to Egypt. ²⁹Some time later, Reuben returned to get Joseph out of the cistern. When he discovered that Joseph was missing, he tore his clothes in grief. ³⁰Then he went back to his brothers and lamented, "The boy is gone! What will I do now?"

"Act out being sad that Joseph was gone."

³⁶Meanwhile, the Midianite traders arrived in Egypt, where they sold Joseph to Potiphar, an officer of Pharaoh, the king of Egypt. Potiphar was captain of the palace guard.

THE Jesus CONNECTION

When we feel angry, we can talk to Jesus, and Jesus will help us do the right thing.

Let's Talk

Cuddles says,
"Let's talk about feelings!!"

- What makes you mad?
- What do you think God wants you to do when you feel mad or frustrated?

Hold It!

This week when your child shows signs of anger or frustration, say, "Hold it! Let's talk about how you feel." Ask your child to describe his or her feelings, and share how God might want us to behave when we feel that way.

Prayer Chart

Make a feelings chart with a square for every day this week and the title "Today I Feel . . ." Encourage your child to fill in the square for each day with a picture that shows his or her emotions. Discuss what Joseph's brothers felt and how God can help us do what's right no matter how we feel.

Pockets says,
"It's time to pray!"

Dear God, thank you that we can come to you any time, even with angry feelings. Please help us to talk to you and trust you to help us do what's right. In Jesus' name, amen.

Joseph Forgives

Genesis 42, 45

"Make your very best bow."

Since Joseph was governor of all Egypt and in charge of selling grain to all the people, it was to him that his brothers came. When they arrived, they bowed before him with their faces to the ground. [7]Joseph recognized his brothers instantly, but he pretended to be a stranger and spoke harshly to them. "Where are you from?" he demanded.

His Brothers

"From the land of Canaan," they replied. "We have come to buy food."

[1]Joseph could stand it no longer. There were many people in the room, and he said to his attendants, "Out, all of you!" So he was alone

with his brothers when he told them who he was. ²Then he broke down and wept. He wept so loudly the Egyptians could hear him, and word of it quickly carried to Pharaoh's palace.

³"I am Joseph!" he said to his brothers. "Is my father still alive?" But his brothers

"Pretend to cry."

were speechless!
They were
stunned to realize that
Joseph was standing there
in front of them. ⁴"Please, come closer,"
he said to them. So they came closer. And he
said again, "I am Joseph, your brother, whom
you sold into slavery in Egypt. ⁵But don't be
upset, and don't be angry with yourselves for
selling me to this place. It was God who sent
me here ahead of you to preserve your lives.
⁶This famine that has ravaged the land for
two years will last five more years, and there
will be neither plowing nor harvesting.

"Pretend to pick
plants until
you can't find
any more."

"Move your finger along the map to show the path Joseph took to Egypt."

[7] God has sent me ahead of you to keep you and your families alive and to preserve many survivors. [8] So it was God who sent me here, not you! And he is the one who made me an adviser to Pharaoh—the manager of his entire palace and the governor of all Egypt.

[15] Then Joseph kissed each of his brothers and wept over them, and after that they began talking freely with him.

THE
Jesus
CONNECTION Just as Joseph forgave his brothers,

Dear God, help us remember to be like Joseph and forgive people who say and do things that hurt us and make us feel bad. In Jesus' name, amen.

Let's Talk

- Tell about a time someone hurt your feelings.
- How can you forgive when someone hurts your feelings?

Pockets says, "It's time to pray!"

Table Talk

As you eat dinner with your family this week, talk about how Joseph helped his brothers get food to eat. Then think of ways you can show love to people who have made you feel bad.

Finger Play

Act out forgiveness by doing a finger play. Crook your index finger and say, "I'm so sorry. I didn't mean to make you feel bad." Let your child wiggle a finger and answer, "I forgive you." Then intertwine your fingers for a finger hug. Reverse roles throughout the week when either of you needs forgiveness.

Cuddles says, "Let's forgive!"

Jesus will forgive us for anything we've done wrong if we ask him to.

God Protects

About this time, a man and woman from the tribe of Levi got married. ²The woman became pregnant and gave birth to a son. She saw that he was a special baby and kept him hidden for three months. ³But when she could no longer hide him, she got a basket made of

Baby Moses

Exodus 2:1-10

papyrus reeds and waterproofed it with tar and pitch. She put the baby in the basket and laid it among the reeds along the bank of the Nile River.

"Pretend you're riding in a basket in the water, rocking back and forth."

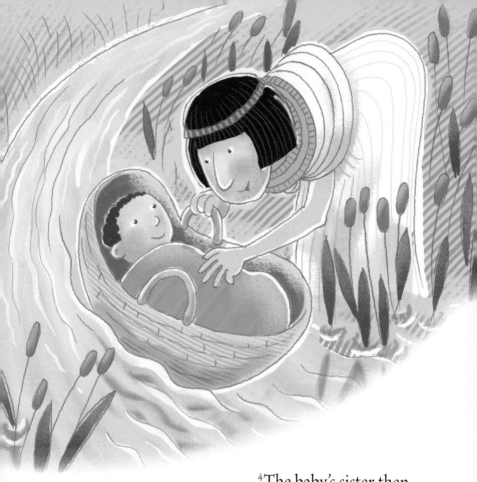

"Show how
a baby cries."

⁴The baby's sister then stood at a distance, watching to see what would happen to him.

⁵Soon Pharaoh's daughter came down to bathe in the river, and her attendants walked along the riverbank. When the princess saw the basket among the reeds, she sent her maid to get it for her. ⁶When the princess opened it, she saw the baby. The little boy was crying,

and she felt
sorry for him.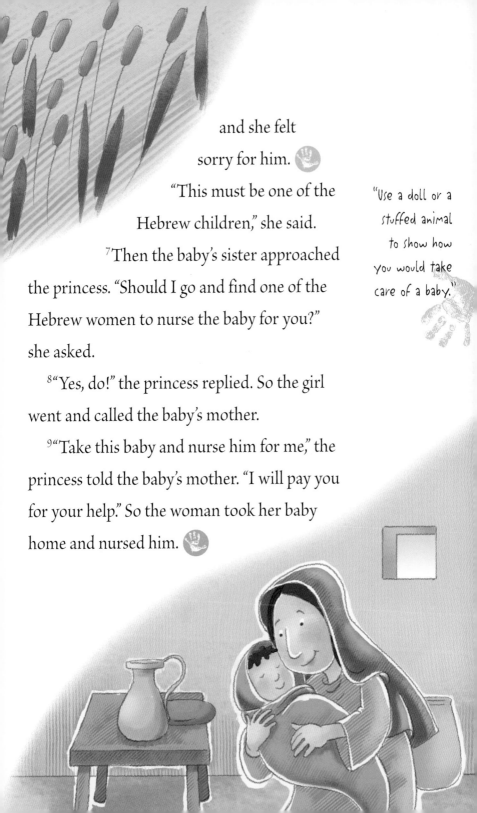
"This must be one of the
Hebrew children," she said.

⁷Then the baby's sister approached
the princess. "Should I go and find one of the
Hebrew women to nurse the baby for you?"
she asked.

⁸"Yes, do!" the princess replied. So the girl
went and called the baby's mother.

⁹"Take this baby and nurse him for me," the
princess told the baby's mother. "I will pay you
for your help." So the woman took her baby
home and nursed him.

"Use a doll or a
stuffed animal
to show how
you would take
care of a baby."

¹⁰Later, when the boy was older, his mother brought him back to Pharaoh's daughter, who adopted him as her own son. The princess named him Moses, for she explained, "I lifted him out of the water."

THE Jesus CONNECTION

God took care of Baby Moses. God took care of Baby Jesus, too, so he could grow up and help us every day!

Float the Boat

This week let your bathtub become the Nile River. Place a small toy inside a plastic cup, and let your child safely sail "Baby Moses" down the river. Talk about how God took care of Baby Moses and how God takes care of us.

Cuddles says, "Let's float a boat!"

Let's Sing

Sing this song with your child to the tune of "Row, Row, Row Your Boat."

**God takes care of me
Every single day.
I will always trust in him
As I work and play.**

Pockets says, "It's time to pray!"

Let's Talk

• What do people do to take care of you?
• Tell about a time someone helped you when you were scared or sad.

Dear God, thank you for sending people to take care of Moses. Thank you for sending lots of people to love and care for [child's name], too!

In Jesus' name, amen.

Moses and the

One day Moses was tending the flock of his father-in-law, Jethro, the priest of Midian. He led the flock far into the wilderness and came to Sinai, the mountain of God. ²There the angel of the LORD appeared to him in a blazing fire from the middle of a bush. Moses stared in amazement. Though the bush was engulfed in flames, it didn't burn up. ³"This is amazing," Moses said to himself. "Why isn't that bush burning up? I must go see it."

"'Baa' like one of Moses' sheep."

Burning Bush

[4]When the LORD saw Moses coming to take a closer look, God called to him from the middle of the bush, "Moses! Moses!"

"Here I am!" Moses replied.

[5]"Do not come any closer," the LORD

"Cup your hands around your mouth and say, 'Moses! Moses!'"

"Take off your shoes and socks, and walk around as if you're standing on a special place."

warned. "Take off your sandals, for you are standing on holy ground. ⁶I am the God of your father—the God of Abraham, the God of Isaac, and the God of Jacob." When Moses heard this, he covered his face because

"Cover your face with your hands."

74

he was afraid to
look at God.

⁷Then the LORD
told him, "I have certainly
seen the oppression of my people in
Egypt. I have heard their cries of distress
because of their harsh slave drivers. Yes,
I am aware of their suffering. ⁸So I have come
down to rescue them from the power of the
Egyptians and lead them out of Egypt into
their own fertile and spacious land. It is a
land flowing with milk and honey—the land
where the Canaanites, Hittites, Amorites,
Perizzites, Hivites, and Jebusites now live.

"Pretend you're
drinking milk
and eating sweet
honey. Think about
God's promise of
a land where cows
gave milk and
bees made honey."

⁹Look! The cry of the people of Israel has reached me, and I have seen how harshly the Egyptians abuse them. ¹⁰Now go, for I am sending you to Pharaoh. You must lead my people Israel out of Egypt."

"Play follow the Leader with me."

THE
Jesus
CONNECTION   A burning bush was a pretty amazing

Let's Talk

- What are some things God wants you to do? When is it hard for you to obey?
- Why does God want you to obey him?

Dear God, teach us to listen to your voice. Please help us to obey and go wherever you say to go. In Jesus' name, amen.

Pockets says, "It's time to pray!"

Burning Bush

This week, help your child draw a bush on cardboard and glue some grass to it. Cut out small strips of orange and red paper, and have your child glue them onto the bush while you discuss how God spoke to Moses from a burning bush. Hang the bush in a special place so your child will be reminded to listen to God.

Be a Leader!

One night at bedtime, play Simon Says. As you help your child complete bedtime tasks, name tasks to do and throw in some silly ones without the words "Simon says." Remind your child that God gives us good things to do. God told Moses what to do, and Moses obeyed. We can obey God too!

Cuddles says, "Let's play Simon Says!"

thing. Here's an even *more* amazing thing: Jesus loves you all the time!

God Parts

Then Moses raised his hand over the sea, and the LORD opened up a path through the water with a strong east wind. The wind blew all that night, turning the seabed into dry land. ²²So the people of Israel walked through the middle of the sea on dry ground, with walls of water on each side!

"Walk around the room and pretend you're walking between walls of water."

the Red Sea

Exodus 14:21-29

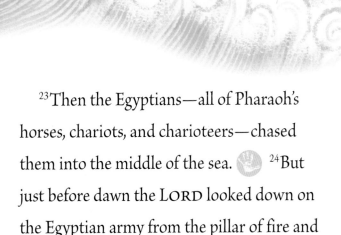

²³Then the Egyptians—all of Pharaoh's horses, chariots, and charioteers—chased them into the middle of the sea. ²⁴But just before dawn the LORD looked down on the Egyptian army from the pillar of fire and

"Pretend you're running from Pharaoh's army."

"Run the other direction."

cloud, and he threw their forces into total confusion. ²⁵He twisted their chariot wheels, making their chariots difficult to drive. "Let's get out of here—away from these Israelites!" the Egyptians shouted. "The LORD is fighting for them against Egypt!"

²⁶When all the Israelites had reached the other side, the LORD said to Moses, "Raise

your hand over
the sea again. Then the
waters will rush back and
cover the Egyptians and their chariots
and charioteers." 🤚 ²⁷So as the sun began to
rise, Moses raised his hand over the sea, and
the water rushed back into its usual place. The
Egyptians tried to escape, but the LORD swept
them into the sea. ²⁸Then the waters returned
and covered all the chariots and charioteers—
the entire army of Pharaoh. Of all the

"Raise your
hand as high
as you can."

Egyptians who had chased the Israelites into the sea, not a single one survived.

²⁹But the people of Israel had walked through the middle of the sea on dry ground, as the water stood up like a wall on both sides.

"Pretend you are one of the bad people trying to swim in deep water."

THE Jesus CONNECTION

God showed how powerful he is when he parted the Red Sea—and when he brought Jesus back to life!

Parting the Water

Cuddles says, "Let's blow bubbles!"

In the tub this week, encourage your child to blow really hard on the surface of the water and try to make it split into two parts. Remind your child that while all we can do is blow bubbles, God is much stronger and more powerful. He made a whole sea split in two!

Split-Sea Snack

Make some vanilla pudding, dyed blue with food coloring. As you eat it with your child, use your spoons to make dry paths through the pudding. Talk about God's miracle of splitting the Red Sea.

Pockets says, "It's time to pray!"

Let's Talk

- Who are some people who keep you safe?
- What amazing things can our strong God do?

Dear God, please keep us safe. And help us to see how strong and powerful you are. In Jesus' name, amen.

The Ten Commandments

Exodus 20

Then God gave the people all these instructions: ²"I am the LORD your God, who rescued you from the land of Egypt, the place of your slavery. ³"You must not have any other god but me. ⁴"You must not make for yourself an idol of any kind or an image of anything in the heavens or on the earth or in the sea.

⁷ "You must

"God said not to do things that show we don't respect him. Shake your head no three times."

not misuse
the name of
the LORD your
God. The LORD
will not let you go
unpunished if you
misuse his name.

⁸"Remember to
observe the Sabbath
day by keeping it holy. ⁹You
have six days each week for your
ordinary work, ¹⁰but the seventh day is a
Sabbath day of rest dedicated to the
LORD your God. On that day
no one in your household
may do any work.

"Name two things
you think God
wants us to do
on Sundays."

"Give an 'honor hug' and promise to listen to the person who's reading to you!"

¹²"Honor your father and mother. Then you will live a long, full life in the land the LORD your God is giving you.

¹³"You must not murder.

¹⁴"You must not commit adultery.

¹⁵"You must not steal.

¹⁶"You must not testify falsely against your neighbor.

¹⁷"You must not covet your neighbor's house. You must not covet your neighbor's wife, male or female servant, ox or donkey, or anything else that belongs to your neighbor."

"Sit on your hands."

"Practice telling the truth right now. Tell something true about a friend."

"These are God's ten rules called the Ten Commandments. Count to ten on your fingers."

THE Jesus CONNECTION God wants us to obey

Sing-Along Time

Cuddles says, "Let's sing!"

Look for the number "10" on signs with your child this week. When you see it, sing this song together to the tune of "Are You Sleeping?":

God's commandments,
God's commandments—
There are ten. There are ten.
Yes, I will obey them. Yes, I will obey them.
I love God. I love God.

Dos and Don'ts

Play a commandments game with your child where you give "do" commands like, "Do hop three times" and "don't" commands like "Don't giggle." Remind your child that obeying God's commandments helps us get along with him and with others.

Let's Talk

- What are some ways you can obey the Ten Commandments?
- What do you think God would like you to do when you want to disobey?

Pockets says, "It's time to pray!"

Dear God, help us obey your rules and remember to respect you. In Jesus' name, amen.

his commands. Jesus obeyed God in everything he did!

The 12

Numbers 13

"How many spies can you count on this page?"

The LORD now said to Moses, [2]"Send out men to explore the land of Canaan, the land I am giving to the Israelites. Send one leader from each of the twelve ancestral tribes." [3]So Moses did as the LORD commanded him. He sent out twelve men, all tribal leaders of Israel, from their camp in the wilderness of Paran.

Spies Explore

²¹So they went up and explored the land
from the wilderness of Zin as far as Rehob, near
Lebo-hamath. ²³When they came to the valley
of Eshcol, they cut down a branch with a single

cluster of grapes so large that it took two of them to carry it on a pole between them! They also brought back samples of the pomegranates and figs.

²⁷This was their report
to Moses: "We entered the land you sent
us to explore, and it is indeed a bountiful
country—a land flowing with milk and honey.
Here is the kind of fruit it produces. ²⁸But the
people living there are powerful, and their
towns are large and fortified. We even saw
giants there, the descendants of Anak!

"Jump as high as
you can. A giant
is even taller
than that!"

²⁹The Amalekites live in the Negev, and the Hittites, Jebusites, and Amorites live in the hill country. The Canaanites live along the coast of the Mediterranean Sea and along the Jordan Valley."

³⁰But Caleb tried to quiet the people as they stood before Moses. "Let's go at once to take the land," he said. "We can certainly conquer it!"

"Put your hands on your hips to show how you look when you're brave."

THE
Jesus
CONNECTION   God prepared a place for the people

92

Let's Talk

- What are some places that are scary to you?
- What can you say to God when you're in a new place and feeling scared?

Dear God, please help us when we're scared. **In Jesus' name, amen.**

Pockets says, "It's time to pray!"

Fabulous Fruits

At the grocery store this week, explore the produce section with your child to find new fruits, like figs or pomegranates. Find the biggest fruit you can! Talk about how God put big fruit in the land where the Israelites would live someday.

Exploration

Pretend you're seeing and exploring your backyard or neighborhood for the first time, and tell about the amazing things you see and discover. Talk about how the spies explored a new land.

Cuddles says, "Let's explore!"

f Israel. Jesus is preparing a special place for us in heaven!

Balaam's

Balaam got up, saddled his donkey, and started off with the Moabite officials. [22] But God was angry that Balaam was going, so he sent the angel of the LORD to stand in the road to block his way. As Balaam and two servants were riding along, [23] Balaam's donkey saw the

"Make donkey sounds. 'Hee-haw!'"

Talking Donkey

Numbers 22:21-31

angel of the LORD standing in the road with a drawn sword in his hand. The donkey bolted off the road into a field, but Balaam beat it and turned it back onto the road. ²⁴Then the angel of the LORD stood at a place where the road

"The angel was trying to block Balaam's path. Stand in a doorway, and try to block me from getting through."

narrowed between two vineyard walls.  ²⁵When the donkey saw the angel of the LORD, it tried to squeeze by and crushed Balaam's foot against the wall. So Balaam beat the donkey again. ²⁶Then the angel of the LORD moved farther down the road and stood in a place too narrow for the donkey to get by at all. ²⁷This time when the donkey saw the angel, it lay down under

Balaam. In a fit of
rage Balaam beat the
animal again with his staff.

"What would
you think if a
donkey started
talking? Make a
surprised face."

²⁸Then the LORD gave the donkey
the ability to speak. "What have I done to you
that deserves your beating me three times?"
it asked Balaam.

²⁹"You have made me look like a fool!"
Balaam shouted. ³⁰"But I am the same donkey
you have ridden all your life," the donkey
answered. "Have I ever done anything like
this before?"

"No," Balaam admitted.

"We worship God by saying nice things to him. What nice things do you want to say to God?"

³¹Then the LORD opened Balaam's eyes, and he saw the angel of the LORD standing in the roadway with a drawn sword in his hand. Balaam bowed his head and fell face down on the ground before him.

THE Jesus CONNECTION

Balaam finally did what God wanted him to do. Jesus teaches us how to obey God right away.

Sock Donkey

Help your child stuff an old sock with stuffing or crumpled paper. Tie up the end with string that hangs down like a tail. Let your child decorate the sock to look like a donkey that's lying down. Throughout the week, make the donkey talk to help your child remember to obey.

Cuddles says, "Let's make a donkey!"

Talking Back

Using stuffed animals, role-play with your child the parts of Balaam and the donkey, where they have a conversation about why Balaam is hurting her. Take turns with each role. Talk about what it would be like if animals really talked.

Pockets says, "It's time to pray!"

Let's Talk

• What things does God tell us to do?
• Why is it important to do what God wants?

Lord, help us to do what's right. Help us to listen to you, obey you, and worship you. In Jesus' name, amen.

Jericho's

Joshua 6

The gates of Jericho were tightly shut because the people were afraid of the Israelites. No one was allowed to go out or in. ²But the LORD said to Joshua, "I have given you Jericho, its king, and all its strong warriors. ³You and your fighting men should march around the town once a day for six days. ⁴Seven priests will walk ahead of the Ark, each carrying a ram's horn. On the seventh day you are to march around the town

"March your fingers around the wall in the picture!"

Falling Walls

"Count to seven."

seven times, with the priests blowing the horns. ⁵When you hear the priests give one long blast on the rams' horns, have all the people shout as loud as they can. Then the walls of the town will collapse, and the people can charge straight into the town."

"Ready to shout? Let's do it!"

[20]When the people heard the sound of the rams' horns, they shouted as loud as they could. Suddenly, the walls of Jericho collapsed, and the Israelites charged straight into the town and captured it.

"Stand up straight like a wall. Then fall to the ground."

Pockets says, "It's time to pray!"

Dear God, you did an amazing thing when your people obeyed you and you made those walls fall down. Thank you for doing amazing things for us when we obey you too. In Jesus' name, amen.

Let's Talk

• What do you need God's help with right now?
• When is it hard for you to obey?

THE Jesus CONNECTION God knocked down the

Falling Walls

Build a block wall with your child, and march around it seven times. Then let your child knock it over! Remember that God helped his people by knocking down walls, and God will help you, too.

Cuddles says,
"Let's build!"

Praise Parade

Show your child how to make a horn by cupping your hand around your mouth. Blow on your horn every time you see something amazing that God does this week!

walls of Jericho so his people could get inside the city. God sent Jesus so we can trust him and get into heaven!

Gideon's Sign

"Stand tall with hands on hips to look like a superhero."

The angel of the LORD came and sat beneath the great tree at Ophrah, which belonged to Joash of the clan of Abiezer. Gideon son of Joash was threshing wheat at the bottom of a winepress to hide the grain from the Midianites. ¹²The angel of the

LORD appeared to him and said, "Mighty hero, the LORD is with you!"

¹³"Sir," Gideon replied, "if the LORD is with us, why has all this happened to us? And where are all the miracles our ancestors told us about?

Didn't they say, 'The LORD brought us up out of Egypt'? But now the LORD has abandoned us and handed us over to the Midianites."

¹⁴Then the LORD turned to him and said, "Go with the strength you have, and rescue Israel from the Midianites. I am sending you!"

"Show your muscles!"

¹⁵"But Lord," Gideon replied, "how can I rescue Israel? My clan is the weakest in the whole tribe of Manasseh, and I am the least in my entire family!"

¹⁶The LORD said to him, "I will be with you. And you will destroy the Midianites as if you were fighting against one man."

³⁶Then Gideon said to God, "If you are truly going to use me to rescue Israel as you promised, ³⁷prove it to me in this way. I will put a wool fleece on the threshing floor tonight.

"March around the room, and stick with me."

If the fleece is wet with dew in the morning but the ground is dry, then I will know that you are going to help me rescue Israel as you promised." ³⁸ And that is just what happened. When Gideon got up early the next morning, he squeezed the fleece and wrung out a whole bowlful of water.

"Squeeze a sheet or blanket, and pretend water is coming out of it."

THE
Jesus
CONNECTION

Let's Talk

- What are some things you want to do that you would have to be really strong to do?
- What are some ways God lets you know that he is with you?

Dear God, thank you that you're always with us and that you make us strong. Help us be strong for you. In Jesus' name, amen.

Pockets says, "It's time to pray!"

God Is Here

Wherever you spend time this week (at home, at a park, store, library, school, and so on), say with your child, "God is here!" Talk about how God promised he would be with Gideon and how God is always with us, too.

Wet Cloths

When your child is in the tub this week, hang several washcloths on the side of the tub. Ask your child about the wool cloth that Gideon left on the ground. Then put the cloths in the tub and let your child wring out the water as you talk about how God shows he is with you by helping you.

Cuddles says, "Let's play!"

God was with Gideon. And God wanted to be with us so much that he sent Jesus to earth!

Ruth Stays

"Take giant steps around the room, and pretend you're carrying a suitcase and moving from Bethlehem to Moab."

I n the days when the judges ruled in Israel, a severe famine came upon the land. So a man from Bethlehem in Judah left his home and went to live in the country of Moab, taking his wife and two sons with him. ²The man's name was Elimelech, and his wife was Naomi.

110

with Naomi

Ruth 1

Their two sons were Mahlon and Kilion. They were Ephrathites from Bethlehem in the land of Judah. And when they reached Moab, they settled there.

³Then Elimelech died, and Naomi was left

"Sad things happened to Naomi. Show me a sad face."

with her
two sons. ⁴The two
sons married Moabite women.
One married a woman named Orpah, and
the other a woman named Ruth. But about
ten years later, ⁵both Mahlon and Kilion died.
This left Naomi alone, without her two sons or
her husband.

⁶Then Naomi heard in Moab that the
LORD had blessed his people in Judah by
giving them good crops again. So Naomi and

her daughters-in-law got ready to leave Moab to return to her homeland. ⁷With her two daughters-in-law she set out from the place where she had been living, and they took the road that would lead them back to Judah.

⁸But on the way, Naomi said to her two daughters-in-law, "Go back to your mothers' homes. And may the LORD reward you for your kindness to your husbands and to me."

¹⁶But Ruth replied, "Don't ask me to leave you and turn back. Wherever you go, I will go; wherever

"Use baby steps, and pretend to walk quietly back to Bethlehem."

"follow me around the room, and walk like I do."

you live, I will live. Your people will be my people, and your God will be my God. ¹⁷Wherever you die, I will die, and there I will be buried. May the LORD punish me severely if I allow anything but death to separate us!" ¹⁸When Naomi saw that Ruth was determined to go with her, she said nothing more.

THE Jesus CONNECTION

Ruth followed Naomi and worshiped her God. We can follow Jesus and worship him!

Travel Time

Whenever you travel together by car, bus, or train this week, name places where you like to go with your family. Talk about staying close to your family and to God wherever you go—just like Ruth did.

Cuddles says, "Let's go for a ride!"

Story Song

Teach your child the following song to the tune of "The Farmer in the Dell":

Ruth stayed with Naomi. *(Hold both index fingers up, apart.)*

Ruth stayed with Naomi. *(Move fingers together.)*

Naomi moved to Bethlehem. *(Move your right index finger forward.)*

Ruth stayed with Naomi. *(Move your left index finger to meet the right.)*

Pockets says, "It's time to pray!"

Let's Talk

- What are some ways you're a helpful family member like Ruth?
- What are some things you love about the people in your family?

Dear God, we know it's important to love the people in our families. Help our family follow you wherever you lead us. In Jesus' name, amen.

Boaz Helps

Ruth 2:15-22

When Ruth went back to work again, Boaz ordered his young men, "Let her gather grain right among the sheaves without stopping her. [16] And pull out some heads of barley from the bundles and drop them on purpose for her. Let her pick them up, and don't give her a hard time!"

[17] So Ruth gathered barley there all day, and when she beat out the grain that evening, it

"Pretend you're gathering grain like Ruth did."

116

Ruth

filled an entire basket. [18] She carried it back into town and showed it to her mother-in-law. Ruth also gave her the roasted grain that was left over from her meal.

[19]"Where did you gather all this grain

"Pretend you're eating your favorite meal."

117

today?" Naomi asked. "Where did you work? May the LORD bless the one who helped you!"

So Ruth told her mother-in-law about the man in whose field she had worked. She said, "The man I worked with today is named Boaz."

²⁰ "May the LORD bless him!" Naomi told her daughter-in-law. "He is showing his kindness to us as well as to your dead husband. That man is one of our closest relatives, one of our family redeemers."

²¹ Then Ruth said, "What's more, Boaz even told me to come back and stay with his harvesters until the entire harvest is completed."

"Boaz showed kindness to Ruth. Be kind by saying something nice to me."

[22]"Good!" Naomi exclaimed. "Do as he said, my daughter. Stay with his young women right through the whole harvest. You might be harassed in other fields, but you'll be safe with him."

"Name three people who make you feel safe."

THE
Jesus
CONNECTION God sent Boaz to be kind to Ruth

Let's Talk

- What are some ways people have been kind to you?
- What kind things can you do for a friend this week?

Dear God, help us to be kind, just as Boaz was kind to Ruth. In Jesus' name, amen.

Pockets says, "It's time to pray!"

Kindness Counts

Hang up a blank piece of paper, and draw a heart on it each time you see your child being kind this week. Encourage your child to fill the page with hearts, and congratulate your child for all the hearts on the paper at the end of the week.

Clean Up

When it's time for your child to clean up toys this week, help gather the toys, and talk about how Ruth picked up the grain and put it in a basket. For each toy you put away, name a way you can be kind to someone.

Cuddles says, "Let's gather toys!"

and help her. God sent Jesus to be kind and help *you!*

Samuel Hears God

1 Samuel 3:1-10

Meanwhile, the boy Samuel served the LORD by assisting Eli. Now in those days messages from the LORD were very rare, and visions were quite uncommon.

²One night Eli, who was almost blind by now, had gone to bed. ³The lamp of God had not yet gone out, and Samuel was sleeping

"Put one hand behind your ear, and when I say, 'Samuel,' raise your hand in the air."

in the Tabernacle near the Ark of God. [4]Suddenly the LORD called out, "Samuel!"

"Yes?" Samuel replied. "What is it?" [5]He got up and ran to Eli. "Here I am. Did you call me?"

"I didn't call you," Eli replied. "Go back to bed." So he did.

[6]Then the LORD called out again, "Samuel!" Again Samuel got up and went to Eli. "Here I am. Did you call me?"

"I didn't call you, my son," Eli said. "Go back to bed." [7]Samuel did not yet know the LORD

"Pretend to sleep. Then sit up as fast as you can when I say your name."

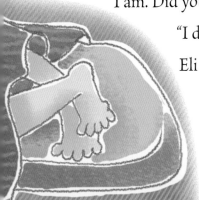

123

"Get up and walk across the room, and then come back to me."

because he had never had a message from the LORD before. ⁸So the LORD called a third time, and once more Samuel got up and went to Eli. "Here I am. Did you call me?"

Then Eli realized it was the LORD who was calling the boy. ⁹So he said to Samuel, "Go and lie down again, and if someone calls again, say, 'Speak, LORD, your servant is listening.'" So Samuel went back to bed.

¹⁰And the LORD came and called as before, "Samuel! Samuel!"

And Samuel replied, "Speak, your servant is listening."

"Listen closely while I whisper something. See if you can hear me."

THE Jesus CONNECTION

Do You Hear What I Hear?

Cuddles says, "Let's listen!"

Go on a walk as a family and listen. Don't talk except to name sounds you hear while you walk. After the walk, talk about how we can listen to God.

Name That Sound

Select noise-making items from around your house, such as a kitchen timer, a pen that clicks, or a container with a lid. Have your child close his or her eyes and try to identify each item from the sound it makes. Talk about what God's voice sounds like to you.

Let's Talk

• What are some things God tells us to do?
• If you heard God say something out loud, what do you think his voice would sound like?

Pockets says, "It's time to pray!"

Dear God, help us to pay attention when you talk to us, just as Samuel listened when you called. In Jesus' name, amen.

Jesus said people who follow him know his voice.
Jesus wants us to listen to him and follow him!

Goliath stood and shouted a taunt across to the Israelites. "Why are you all coming out to fight?" he called. "I am the Philistine champion, but you are only the servants of Saul. Choose one man to come down here and fight me!"

[32] "Don't worry about this Philistine," David

Wins

1 Samuel 17

told Saul. "I'll go fight him!"

³³"Don't be ridiculous!" Saul replied. "There's no way you can fight this Philistine and possibly win! You're only a boy, and he's been a man of war since his youth."

"Goliath was really tall, and David was small. Point to two places on the wall to show how tall you think David and Goliath were."

127

"Make lion and bear sounds."

³⁴But David persisted. "I have been taking care of my father's sheep and goats," he said. "When a lion or a bear comes to steal a lamb from the flock, ³⁵I go after it with a club and rescue the lamb from its mouth. If the animal turns on me, I catch it by the jaw and club it to death. ³⁶I have done this to both lions and bears, and I'll do it to this pagan Philistine, too, for he has defied the armies of the living God!

³⁷The LORD who rescued me from the claws of the lion and the bear will rescue me from this Philistine!"

Saul finally consented. "All right, go ahead," he said. "And may the LORD be with you!"

⁴⁰He picked up five smooth stones from a stream and put them into his shepherd's bag. Then, armed only with his shepherd's staff and sling, he started across the valley to fight the Philistine.

"Use your fingers to count to five."

"Put a finger on your forehead, and then lie down on the floor."

⁴⁸As Goliath moved closer to attack, David quickly ran out to meet him. ⁴⁹Reaching into his shepherd's bag and taking out a stone, he hurled it with his sling and hit the Philistine in the forehead. The stone sank in, and Goliath stumbled and fell face down on the ground.

THE Jesus CONNECTION

Jesus said we'd have problems, but he also said he's stronger than our problems!

Little Rocks

Cuddles says, "Let's pick up rocks!"

Next time you're outside, have each family member find a small rock. Talk about how little the rock was that brought down the big giant and some of the ways that God can use a little boy or girl to do great things.

Target Toss

Crumple pieces of paper into pretend stones. Choose a high spot on a wall, and try to hit it with the paper stones. Talk about how God was with David and how you know God is with you.

Pockets says, "It's time to pray!"

Let's Talk

• What's a big problem you've had?
• Tell about how you faced that problem.

Dear God, please help us when we have problems that seem as big as giants. Thank you that you're always with us. In Jesus' name, amen.

131

Jonathan and

1 Samuel 18:1-4

"Pretend we're meeting for the first time. We can shake hands and say our names."

David Are Friends

After David had finished talking with Saul, he met Jonathan, the king's son.  There was an immediate bond between them, for Jonathan loved David. ²From that day on Saul kept David with him and wouldn't let him return home. ³And Jonathan made a solemn pact with David, because he loved him as he loved himself.

"Give me a hug."

"Hug yourself."

133

"Look at the
picture. Point
to the things
Jonathan gave to
his friend David."

[4]Jonathan sealed the pact by taking off his robe and giving it to David, together with his tunic, sword, bow, and belt.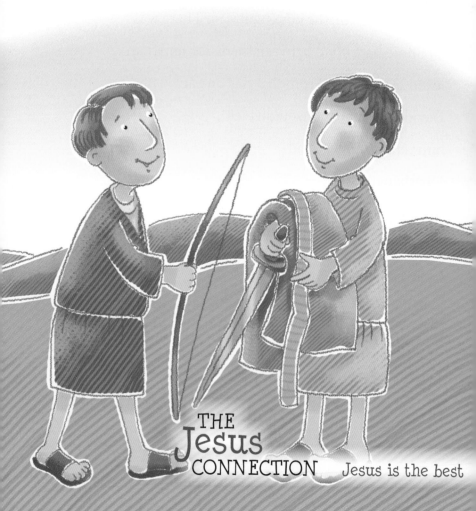

THE
Jesus
CONNECTION   Jesus is the best

Pockets says, "It's time to pray!"

Dear God, thank you for giving us good friends. Help us to be kind to our friends, just like Jonathan and David were. In Jesus' name, amen.

Let's Talk

- What can you do to be a good friend?
- Jonathan gave David his robe. What's the best present a friend ever gave you?

Sharing Friend

The next time your child is playing with a friend or sibling, encourage sharing. Remind your child of how Jonathan shared with David, and encourage your child to tell his or her playmate about Jonathan and David's friendship.

Cuddles says, "Let's be friends!"

Friendship Song

Sing this fun song to the tune of "Did You Ever See a Lassie?" (You can find the tune online if it's unfamiliar.)

Have you ever been a good friend, a good friend, a good friend?
Have you ever been a good friend like Jonathan was?
He shared with his good friend; he's always a good friend.
Have you ever been a good friend like Jonathan was?

friend we could ever have. He's our *forever* friend!

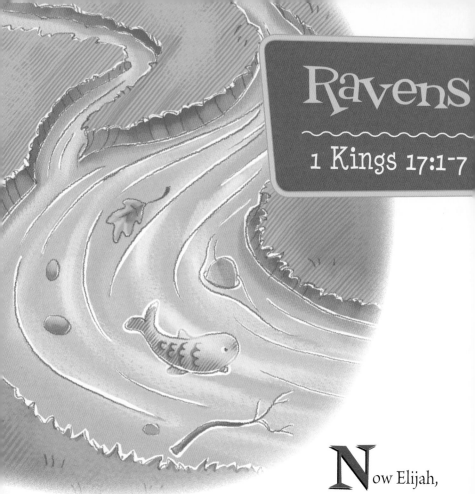

Ravens

1 Kings 17:1-7

"Rub your hands together until they get really warm, like the warm, dry weather in Elijah's land."

Now Elijah, who was from Tishbe in Gilead, told King Ahab, "As surely as the LORD, the God of Israel, lives—the God I serve—there will be no dew or rain during the next few years until I give the word!"

²Then the LORD said to Elijah, ³"Go to the east and hide by Kerith Brook, near where it enters the Jordan River. ⁴Drink from

Feed Elijah

"Act like a raven that God sent to Elijah. Spread your arms, and pretend to fly around the room."

the brook and eat what the ravens bring you, for I have commanded them to bring you food."

⁵So Elijah did as the LORD told him and camped beside Kerith Brook, east of the Jordan.

"Make splashing sounds."

"Pretend you're eating like Elijah. First, reach up to take the food from the birds. Then bend down and take a drink out of the river."

⁶The ravens brought him bread and meat each morning and evening, and he drank from the brook.  ⁷But after a while the brook dried up, for there was no rainfall anywhere in the land.

THE Jesus CONNECTION

God sent ravens with food for Elijah,

Pockets says, "It's time to pray!"

Dear God, thank you for giving us everything we need. Please help us trust you to give us what we need every day. In Jesus' name, amen.

Let's Talk

• If God sent birds to bring you food, what food would you want them to bring?
• What are some things you need that God gives you?

Dinner from the Birds

Cuddles says, "Let's fly!"

One night as you get ready to serve dinner, act like a bird with your child. Let your child help bring the silverware and napkins to the table, and both of you can make bird sounds and have your arms out like you're flying. Talk about how God gave Elijah what he needed by sending birds to feed him.

Water Bank

For one day, each time someone in your family turns on a faucet, that person will shout out, "Thank you, God, for water!" At the end of the day, talk with your child about how great it is that God gives us what we need.

and God sent Jesus to help us have everything we need!

God Feeds a

"Follow me, and we'll pretend to walk to a little village."

Then the LORD said to Elijah, [9]"Go and live in the village of Zarephath, near the city of Sidon. I have instructed a widow there to feed you."

[10]So he went to Zarephath. As he arrived at the gates of the village, he saw a widow gathering sticks, and he asked her, "Would you please bring me a little water in

Widow

a cup?" ¹¹As she was going to get it, he called to her, "Bring me a bite of bread, too."

¹²But she said, "I swear by the LORD your God that I don't have a single piece of bread

"Gather some toys like the widow gathered sticks."

141

"Point to the jar of oil in this picture. Is there a little food or a lot?"

in the house. And I have only a handful of flour left in the jar and a little cooking oil in the bottom of the jug. I was just gathering a few sticks to cook this last meal, and then my son and I will die."

142

¹³But Elijah
said to her, "Don't
be afraid! Go ahead and do
just what you've said, but make a little
bread for me first. Then use what's left to
prepare a meal for yourself and your son.
¹⁴For this is what the LORD, the God of
Israel, says: There will always be flour and
olive oil left in your containers until the
time when the LORD sends rain and the
crops grow again!"

[15] So she did as Elijah said, and she and Elijah and her family continued to eat for many days. [16] There was always enough flour and olive oil left in the containers, just as the LORD had promised through Elijah.

"Pretend you're eating a big meal."

THE
Jesus
CONNECTION   God did a miracle to take

Dear God, thank you for everything you've given us. Thank you for taking care of us, just like you took care of Elijah and the widow. In Jesus' name, amen.

Let's Talk

- What are some things you need that God has given you?
- What's something we need to ask God to give us today?

Pockets says, "It's time to pray!"

Bread Shapes

With your child, sculpt some pieces of soft bread into different fun shapes. Then eat the bread and talk about how God showed Elijah what to do to help the widow and her son have enough food.

God's Helpers

Look for people who need help. Encourage your child to help those people and to tell them that God loves them.

Cuddles says, "Let's help others!"

care of the widow. Jesus does amazing things to take care of us, too!

Then Elijah said to them, "I am the only prophet of the LORD who is left, but Baal has 450 prophets. ²³Now bring two bulls. The prophets of Baal may choose whichever one they wish . . . and lay it on the wood of their altar, but without setting fire to it. I will prepare

God's Power

1 Kings 18

the other bull and lay it on the wood on the altar, but not set fire to it.  ²⁴Then call on the name of your god, and I will call on the name of the LORD. The god who answers by setting fire to the wood is the true God!"

"An altar can be a pile of rocks and sticks. Pretend to stack rocks and sticks, like you're building an altar."

"Cup your hand behind your ear as if you're listening. Then shake your head no."

And all the people agreed.

²⁶So they prepared one of the bulls and placed it on the altar. Then they called on the name of Baal from morning until noontime, shouting, "O Baal, answer us!" But there was no reply of any kind. Then they danced, hobbling around the altar they had made.

²⁹They raved all afternoon until the time of the evening sacrifice, but still there was no sound, no reply, no response.

148

³⁶At the usual time for offering the evening sacrifice, Elijah the prophet walked up to the altar and prayed, "O Lord, God of Abraham, Isaac, and Jacob, prove today that you are God in Israel and that I am your servant. Prove that I have done all this at your command. ³⁷O Lord, answer me! Answer me so these people will know that you, O Lord, are God and that you have brought them back to yourself."

"Pray to God like Elijah did: 'O Lord, answer me.'"

³⁸Immediately the fire of the LORD flashed down from heaven and burned up the young bull, the wood, the stones, and the dust. It even licked up all the water in the trench! ³⁹And when all the people saw it, they fell face down on the ground and cried out, "The LORD—he is God! Yes, the LORD is God!"

THE Jesus CONNECTION

God sent fire to show the people of Israel that he's real. And he sent Jesus to show *us* he's real.

Building Faith

Build a pile of blocks or rocks with your child. If you're able to do this outdoors, pour some water on the pile. Talk about what happened to Elijah's altar and ways you know God is real.

Cuddles says, "Let's build!"

True or False

With your child, look for things that are just pretend, like stuffed animals or play food in a kitchen. Talk about how you know whether something is real or pretend and how you can tell if God is real or pretend.

Pockets says, "It's time to pray!"

Let's Talk

- Tell about something amazing you've seen.
- What does God do that's amazing?

Dear God, help us remember you're the only real God. Show us how real and powerful you are. In Jesus' name, amen.

God Heals

The king of Aram had great admiration for Naaman, the commander of his army, because through him the LORD had given Aram great victories. But though Naaman was a mighty warrior, he suffered from leprosy.

"Leprosy means you have itchy sores all over. Scratch your arms like they itch."

⁹So Naaman went with his horses and chariots and waited at the door of Elisha's house. ¹⁰But Elisha sent a messenger out to

Naaman's Leprosy

him with this message: "Go and wash yourself seven times in the Jordan River. Then your skin will be restored, and you will be healed of your leprosy."

"Pretend to wash your arms."

¹¹But Naaman became angry and stalked

away. "I thought he would certainly come out to meet me!" he said. "I expected him to wave his hand over the leprosy and call on the name of the LORD his God and heal me! 12 Aren't the rivers of Damascus, the Abana and the Pharpar, better than any of the rivers of Israel?

"Make a mad face."

Why shouldn't I wash in them and be healed?" So Naaman turned and went away in a rage.

¹³But his officers tried to reason with him and said, "Sir, if the prophet had told you to do something very difficult, wouldn't you have done it? So you should certainly obey him when he says simply, 'Go and wash and be cured!'" ¹⁴So Naaman went down to the Jordan River and dipped himself seven times, as the man of God had instructed him.

"Count to seven with me."

And his skin became as healthy as the skin of a young child's, and he was healed!

[15]Then Naaman and his entire party went back to find the man of God. They stood before him, and Naaman said, "Now I know that there is no God in all the world except in Israel. So please accept a gift from your servant."

THE
Jesus
CONNECTION Just like God washed

Let's Talk

- What happens when you don't obey your parents? What happens when you do obey?
- Why does God want us to obey him?

Dear God, thank you for healing Naaman's sickness. Please keep us healthy and help us obey you, even if we don't want to. In Jesus' name, amen.

Pockets says, "It's time to pray!"

Seven, Seven, Seven

Give your child a few different actions to repeat seven times. Actions might include "pat your head," "blink," or "say your name." Then talk about seven ways you can obey God this week.

Spotless Bath

Just before your child takes a bath, mark a few spots on his or her hand with a washable marker, or make the spots by putting some bubbles on your child's arm. During the bath, help your child wash off the spots with a washcloth. Remind your child that God washed away Naaman's sickness because Naaman obeyed. Praise your child for a time he or she obeyed you today.

Cuddles says, "Let's splash!"

away Naaman's sores, Jesus washes away bad things we do.

Josiah Fixes

In the eighteenth year of his reign, after he had purified the land and the Temple, Josiah appointed [three men] to repair the Temple of the LORD his God. ⁹They gave Hilkiah the high priest the money that had been collected by the

the Temple

2 Chronicles 34

Levites who served as gatekeepers at the Temple of God. The gifts were brought by people from Manasseh, Ephraim, and from all the remnant of Israel, as well as from all Judah, Benjamin, and the people of Jerusalem.

"Pretend to give me some money to fix the Temple. How much will you give me?"

"Stand up tall like a big building, fall to the ground, and then stand up again!"

¹⁰He entrusted the money to the men assigned to supervise the restoration of the LORD's Temple. Then they paid the workers who did the repairs and renovation of the Temple. ¹¹They hired carpenters and builders, who purchased finished stone for the walls and timber for the rafters and beams. They restored what earlier kings of Judah had allowed to fall into ruin.

¹⁴While they were bringing out the money collected at the LORD's Temple, Hilkiah the priest found the Book of the Law of the LORD that was written by Moses. ¹⁵Hilkiah said to Shaphan the court secretary, "I have found the Book of the Law in the LORD's Temple!" Then Hilkiah gave the scroll to Shaphan.

¹⁶Shaphan took the scroll to the king and reported, "Your officials are doing everything they were assigned to do." ¹⁸Shaphan also told the king, "Hilkiah the priest has given me a scroll." So Shaphan read it to the king.

"Find a big book, and pick it up."

³⁰ And the king went up to the Temple of the LORD with all the people of Judah and Jerusalem, along with the priests and the Levites—all the people from the greatest to the least. There the king read to them the entire Book of the Covenant that had been found in the LORD's Temple.

THE Jesus CONNECTION

The Bible is special because it tells us about Jesus!

Shine and Polish!

The next time you and your child are cleaning up toys or other messes, talk about how Josiah cleaned the Temple. Talk about why it's important to take care of the things God has given us.

Cuddles says, "Let's clean up!"

Build and Rebuild

With your child, cover a Bible with a big pile of blocks. Then dig through the rubble together until you find the Bible. Talk about how Hilkiah found the Bible and what makes the Bible special.

Pockets says, "It's time to pray!"

Let's Talk

- Tell me about a time you lost something that was special to you.
- What makes the Bible a special book?

Dear God, please help us listen to what you say in the Bible and obey you. In Jesus' name, amen.

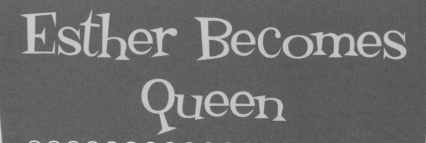

Esther Becomes Queen

Esther 2-5

There was a Jewish man in the fortress of Susa whose name was Mordecai. ⁷This man had a very beautiful and lovely young cousin, Hadassah, who was also called Esther.

¹⁷The king loved Esther more than any of the other young women. He was so delighted with her that he set the royal crown on her head and declared

"Tell me how you like to celebrate your favorite holiday."

her queen instead of Vashti. [18]To celebrate the occasion, he gave a great banquet in Esther's honor for all his nobles and officials, declaring a public holiday for the provinces and giving generous gifts to everyone.

[6]Hathach went out to Mordecai in the square in front of the palace gate. [8]Mordecai gave Hathach a copy of the decree issued in Susa that called for the death of all Jews. [Mordecai] asked Hathach to show it to Esther and explain the situation to her. He also asked Hathach to direct her to go to the king to beg for mercy and plead for her people.

"Mordecai was scared because people wanted to hurt him. Make a scared face."

¹Esther put on her royal robes and entered the inner court of the palace, just across from the king's hall. The king was sitting on his royal throne, facing the entrance. ²When he saw Queen Esther standing there in the inner court, he welcomed her and held out the gold scepter to her. So Esther approached and touched the end of the scepter.

³Then the king asked her, "What do you want, Queen Esther? What is your request? I will give it to you, even if it is half the kingdom!"

"A scepter is a fancy stick for kings and queens. Pretend you're a king or a queen holding a scepter."

THE Jesus CONNECTION Esther had to wait

Royal Robes

Help your child dress like a queen or king. Have your child make a crown to wear. Use a blanket for a royal robe and a large spoon for a scepter. Encourage your child to stay in costume for several activities, like eating and playing. Talk about what makes kings and queens important, and what makes kids important to God.

Hold the Scepter

Help your child wrap a paper towel tube with aluminum foil. Crumple a ball of foil and tape it to the top. Then play a game of Hold the Scepter. The person holding the scepter gets to be king or queen and tells the other people a fun action to do (such as marching in place or singing a song). Only the person holding the scepter can talk.

Let's Talk

• Esther was special to the king. What makes you special?
• What is something you can talk to God about?

Dear God, help us know how special we are to you, just like Queen Esther was special to the king. In Jesus' name, amen.

for permission to see and talk to the king.
But we can talk to King Jesus anytime!

"Tell what you would ask for if a king offered to give you anything."

The king and Haman went to Queen Esther's banquet. ²On this second occasion, while they were drinking wine, the king again said to Esther, "Tell me what you want, Queen Esther. What is your request? I will give it to you, even if it is half the kingdom!"

³Queen Esther replied, "If I have found favor with the king, and if it pleases the king to grant my request, I ask that my life and the lives

168

of my people will be spared. ⁴For my people and I have been sold to those who would kill, slaughter, and annihilate us. If we had merely been sold as slaves, I could remain quiet, for that would be too trivial a matter to warrant disturbing the king."

"Esther was brave to try to save her people, even though talking to the king was scary. Make some muscles."

169

⁵"Who would do such a thing?" King Xerxes demanded. "Who would be so presumptuous as to touch you?"

⁶Esther replied, "This wicked Haman is our adversary and our enemy." Haman grew pale with fright before the king and queen.

¹On that same day King Xerxes gave the property of Haman, the enemy of the Jews, to Queen Esther. Then Mordecai was brought before the king, for Esther had told the king how they were related. ²The king took off his signet ring—which he had taken back from Haman—and gave it to Mordecai. And Esther appointed Mordecai to be in charge of Haman's property.

"Wearing the king's ring gave people power to make rules. Pretend to put on a ring, and tell one rule you'd like to make."

[1] So on March 7 the two decrees of the king were put into effect. On that day, the enemies of the Jews had hoped to overpower them, but quite the opposite happened. It was the Jews who overpowered their enemies.

"Make a loud cheer!"

THE
Jesus
CONNECTION Jesus did something brave too—

172

Dear God, thank you for helping Esther be brave. Please help us be brave and always do the right thing. In Jesus' name, amen.

Let's Talk

- Tell about a time you did something scary.
- When is it hard for you to be brave and do the right thing?

Pockets says, "It's time to pray!"

Be Brave

Help your child do something new this week that takes courage, like travel across the monkey bars, ride a bicycle, tie shoes independently, or eat spinach for the first time. Talk about what it means to stand up for God and bravely do the right thing.

Celebration Time

Choose a night to have a banquet, just as Queen Esther did. Prepare some of your child's favorite foods, use good dishes, decorate with tablecloths and candles, and dine as a royal family! Talk about how Esther was brave at her banquet.

Cuddles says, "Let's have a banquet!"

he died on the cross to forgive us!

The Lord Is

Psalm 23

"find the green meadows and peaceful stream in the picture."

The LORD is my shepherd;
I have all that I need.
²He lets me rest in green meadows;
he leads me beside peaceful streams.
³He renews my strength.
He guides me along
right paths,
bringing honor
to his name.
⁴Even when
I walk
through the
darkest valley,

"Show your muscles."

My Shepherd

"Cover your eyes to make it dark. Then sit really close to me."

I will not be afraid,
    for you are close beside me.
Your rod and your staff
    protect and comfort me.
⁵ You prepare a feast for me
    in the presence of
        my enemies.
You honor me by
    anointing my head
    with oil.

"Pretend to pour a sweet-smelling perfume on my head."

175

"Make a house over your head by putting your arms up like a roof."

My cup overflows with blessings.
⁶ Surely your goodness and unfailing love will
pursue me
all the days of my life,
and I will live in the house of the LORD
forever.

THE Jesus CONNECTION Jesus is called the Good Shepherd.

176

Pockets says, "It's time to pray!"

Dear God, help us remember that you're our Shepherd and you're always close to us, even when we're afraid. In Jesus' name, amen.

Let's Talk

- When are you afraid?
- What can you do the next time you're afraid?

Right Paths

The next time you walk or drive, talk about how the things you pass are like or unlike the green meadows, peaceful stream, and dark valley from Psalm 23. Then talk about how God is with you no matter where you are.

Cuddles says, "Let's go for a walk!"

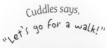

Baa!

With your family, take turns pretending to be shepherds leading the other family members, who are sheep. Talk about ways shepherds care for sheep and ways God takes care of us, his sheep.

Jesus promises that he will always take care of us!

The Fiery

Nebuchadnezzar flew into a rage and ordered that Shadrach, Meshach, and Abednego be brought before him. When they were brought in, [14]Nebuchadnezzar said to them, "Is it true, Shadrach, Meshach, and Abednego, that you refuse to serve my gods

Furnace

Daniel 3

or to worship the gold statue I have set up?"

²⁰Then he ordered some of the strongest men of his army to bind Shadrach, Meshach, and Abednego and throw them into the blazing furnace. ²¹So they tied them up and threw them into the furnace, fully dressed in

"Shake your index finger, and practice saying SHAD-rak, MEE-shack, and a-BED-nee-go."

their pants, turbans, robes, and other garments. ²²And because the king, in his anger, had demanded such a hot fire in the furnace, the flames killed the soldiers as they threw the three men in. ²³So Shadrach, Meshach, and Abednego, securely tied, fell into the roaring flames.

²⁴But suddenly, Nebuchadnezzar jumped up in amazement and exclaimed to his advisers, "Didn't we tie up three men and throw them into the furnace?"

"Hold your hands behind your back like you're tied up."

"Count the people in the furnace."

"Yes, Your Majesty, we certainly did," they replied. ²⁵"Look!" Nebuchadnezzar shouted. "I see four men, unbound, walking around in the fire unharmed! And the fourth looks like a god!"

²⁶Then Nebuchadnezzar came as close as he could to the door of the flaming furnace and shouted: "Shadrach, Meshach, and Abednego, servants of the Most High God, come out! Come here!"

So Shadrach, Meshach, and Abednego stepped out of the fire. ²⁷Then the high officers, officials, governors,

"Find the person in the furnace who looks different from the others."

"Cup your hands to your mouth and shout, 'Come out of the fire!'"

181

"Smell your clothes. They don't smell as if they've been burned, do they?"

and advisers crowded around them and saw that the fire had not touched them. Not a hair on their heads was singed, and their clothing was not scorched. They didn't even smell of smoke!

THE Jesus CONNECTION

A lot of people think the fourth person in the furnace was Jesus! Jesus always stays right beside us wherever we go too.

Jesus and Me

Draw a picture of a time when you wanted to do the right thing, and draw a picture of Jesus next to you, helping you.

Cuddles says, "Let's color!"

Safe in the Fiery Furnace

At bedtime, pretend that the fiery furnace is under your pillow or covers. Gather a few toys and throw them into your "fiery furnace." Then pull them out and notice how they didn't get burned. Talk about how God keeps us safe.

Pockets says, "It's time to pray!"

Let's Talk

- Tell about a time you wanted to disobey but you obeyed instead.
- What are some things that help you know right from wrong?

Dear God, thank you for keeping us safe like you kept Shadrach, Meshach, and Abednego safe. In Jesus' name, amen.

Daniel and the

Daniel 6

The administrators and high officers went to the king and said, "Long live King Darius! ⁷We are all in agreement—we administrators, officials, high officers, advisers, and governors—that the king should make a law that will be strictly enforced. Give orders that for the next thirty days any person who prays to anyone, divine or human—except to you, Your Majesty—will be thrown into the den of lions."

¹⁰But when Daniel learned that the law had been signed, he went home and knelt down as

"Roar like a lion!"

Lions' Den

usual in his upstairs room, with its windows
open toward Jerusalem. He prayed three times a
day, just as he had always done, giving thanks to
his God.

"Fold your hands
and close your
eyes three times."

¹⁶So at last the king gave orders for Daniel to

be arrested and thrown into the den of lions. The king said to him, "May your God, whom you serve so faithfully, rescue you."

¹⁷A stone was brought and placed over the mouth of the den. The king sealed the stone with his own royal seal

and the seals
of his nobles, so
that no one could
rescue Daniel. [18] Then
the king returned to his palace and
spent the night fasting. He refused his
usual entertainment and couldn't sleep at all
that night.

[19] Very early the next morning, the king got
up and hurried out to the lions' den. [20] When
he got there, he called out in anguish, "Daniel,
servant of the living God! Was your God,
whom you serve so faithfully, able to rescue
you from the lions?"

"Fasting means not
eating food. Rub
your tummy like
you're hungry."

²¹Daniel answered, "Long live the king! ²²My God sent his angel to shut the lions' mouths so that they would not hurt me, for I have been found innocent in his sight.  And I have not wronged you, Your Majesty."

²³The king was overjoyed and ordered that Daniel be lifted from the den. Not a scratch was found on him, for he had trusted in his God.

"Pretend to zip your mouth shut."

THE Jesus CONNECTION Daniel trusted God when bad things

Thank you, God, that we can always trust you. Help us to be like Daniel and to trust you when bad things happen. In Jesus' name, amen.

Let's Talk

- Tell about a time you trusted God.
- Where do you like to pray?

Pockets says, "It's time to pray!"

Windows of Praise

This week, sit by a window with your child and pray together. Your prayer might include thanking God, asking for his help, and telling him nice things. Afterward, talk about how Daniel trusted God by praying even when the king said not to.

Faith Walk

Using pillows and chairs, set up an obstacle course, then put a blindfold on your child. Guide your child around the obstacles by saying when to turn, stop, or step over something. Afterward, talk about how God can keep us safe when we trust and obey him.

Cuddles says, "Let's take a walk!"

happened, and we can trust his Son, Jesus, too.

Jonah

T he LORD gave this message to Jonah son of Amitai: ²"Get up and go to the great city of Nineveh. Announce my judgment against it because I have seen how wicked its people are."

³But Jonah got up and went in the opposite direction to get away from the LORD. He went down to the port of Joppa, where he found a ship leaving for Tarshish.

"Quick! Get up and hurry around the room as if you're going to Nineveh!"

"Point to the two signs in the picture."

190

Runs Away

Jonah 1:1-5

"Uh-oh. Jonah tried to hide from God. I'll count to three, and you try to hide from me."

He bought a ticket and went on board, hoping to escape from the LORD by sailing to Tarshish.

⁴But the LORD hurled a powerful wind over the sea, causing a violent storm that threatened to break the ship apart.

"Rock back and forth like you're on a ship in a bad storm."

191

"Make your loudest snoring sounds."

⁵Fearing for their lives, the desperate sailors shouted to their gods for help and threw the cargo overboard to lighten the ship.

But all this time Jonah was sound asleep down in the hold.

THE **Jesus** CONNECTION Jonah learned that

Pockets says, "It's time to pray!"

Dear God, we're sorry about the times we've tried to hide from you. We're glad you love us so much that you never let us get away. In Jesus' name, amen.

Let's Talk

• Jonah disobeyed God. What's a rule you don't like to obey?
• Jonah tried to hide from God. What's something you wouldn't want God to see you do?

Rock and Roll!

For one day, when anyone in your family shouts, "Rock and roll!" re-enact Jonah's storm—no matter where you are. Rock back and forth on the "waves" and make wind sounds. Stomp your feet like thunder.

Cuddles says, "Let's rock!"

Where Is Jonah?

Play Hide and Seek as a family. Talk about how Jonah tried to hide from God, and tell your child that God is always with us, no matter where we go.

he couldn't run away from God. We can't run away from Jesus either.

Jonah and

Then the crew cast lots to see which of them had offended the gods and caused the terrible storm. When they did this, the lots identified Jonah as the culprit. [8]"Why has this awful storm come down on us?" they demanded. "Who are you? What is your line of work?

"Ask a question about me, and I'll ask one about you."

194

the Stormy Sea

Jonah 1:7-17

"Tell why you love God."

What country are you from? What is your nationality?"

⁹Jonah answered, "I am a Hebrew, and I worship the LORD, the God of heaven, who made the sea and the land."

¹⁰The sailors
were terrified when they
heard this, for he had already told them he
was running away from the LORD. "Oh, why
did you do it?" they groaned. ¹¹And since the
storm was getting worse all the time, they
asked him, "What should we do to you to stop
this storm?"

¹²"Throw me into the sea," Jonah said, "and
it will become calm again. I know that this

terrible storm
is all my fault."
¹³Instead, the sailors
rowed even harder to get the
ship to the land. 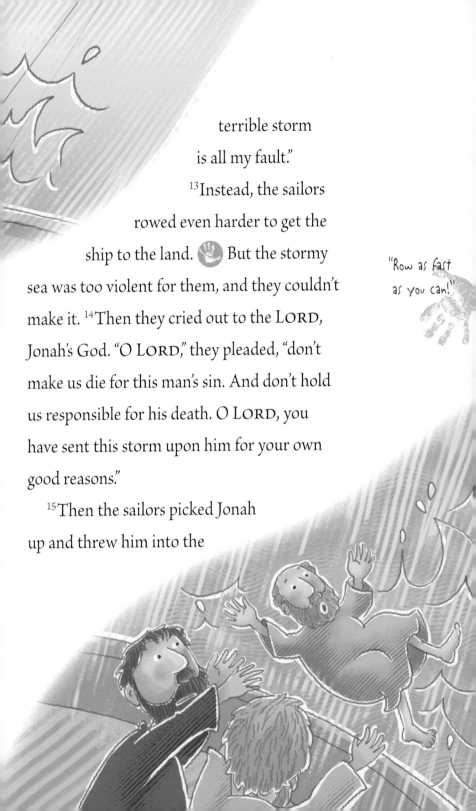 But the stormy
sea was too violent for them, and they couldn't
make it. ¹⁴Then they cried out to the LORD,
Jonah's God. "O LORD," they pleaded, "don't
make us die for this man's sin. And don't hold
us responsible for his death. O LORD, you
have sent this storm upon him for your own
good reasons."

¹⁵Then the sailors picked Jonah
up and threw him into the

"Row as fast
as you can!"

"Pretend to throw someone overboard!"

raging sea, and the storm stopped at once! 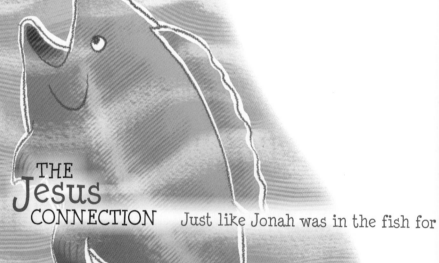 ¹⁶The sailors were awestruck by the LORD's great power, and they offered him a sacrifice and vowed to serve him.

"Stretch your arms out in front of you, and pretend you're a giant fish mouth. See if you can swallow me!"

¹⁷Now the LORD had arranged for a great fish to swallow Jonah. And Jonah was inside the fish for three days and three nights.

THE
Jesus
CONNECTION   Just like Jonah was in the fish for

Overboard!

In the bathtub, use a plastic cup as the ship and an action figure as Jonah. Encourage your child to retell the story of Jonah as much as he or she remembers.

Cuddles says, "Let's go swimming!"

Something Smells Fishy

Eat a tuna sandwich or another kind of fish this week. Smell it before you eat it, and talk about what it might have been like to be swallowed by a fish.

Pockets says, "It's time to pray!"

Let's Talk

- How has someone shown you love when you were in trouble?
- How does God show he cares about us?

Dear God, thank you for sending a fish to swallow Jonah to keep him safe. And thank you for taking care of us! In Jesus' name, amen.

three days, Jesus' body was in a grave for three days. But after three days, Jesus came back to life!

A Fish Swallows Jonah

Jonah 2:1-10

"fold your hands like you're praying."

Then Jonah prayed to the LORD his God from inside the fish.  ²He said,

"I cried out to the LORD in my great trouble,
and he answered me.

I called to you from the land of the dead,
and LORD, you heard me!

³You threw me into the ocean

depths, and I sank down

"Pretend to swim."

to the heart of the sea.

The mighty waters
engulfed me;

I was buried beneath your
wild and stormy waves. 🖐

⁴Then I said, 'O LORD,
you have driven me from your
presence.

Yet I will look once more toward
your holy Temple.'

⁵"I sank beneath the waves,
and the waters closed over me.

Seaweed wrapped itself around my head. ✋

⁶ I sank down to the very roots of the
mountains.

I was imprisoned in the earth,
whose gates lock shut forever.

But you, O LORD my God,
snatched me from the jaws of death! 🖐

"Wrap your arm
around your head,
and pretend your
arm is seaweed."

"Hug yourself
tightly, and
imagine God
holding you."

"Put your hand
to your ear."

⁷As my life was

slipping away,

    I remembered the LORD.

    And my earnest prayer

went out to you

    in your holy Temple.

    ⁸Those who worship

false gods

    turn their backs on all

God's mercies.

    ⁹But I will offer sacrifices

to you with songs of praise,

    and I will fulfill all my vows.

For my salvation comes from the LORD

alone."

    ¹⁰Then the LORD ordered the fish to spit

Jonah out onto the beach.

"Jump like you're getting spit out onto the beach."

THE Jesus CONNECTION God sent a fish to save Jonah,

Fish Tag

Say, "Into the water, Jonah was sinking. But God sent a fish, so he'd do some thinking." Then chase your child. When you catch your child, playfully lift your child and say, "I caught you! I caught you! You won't get drowned. I'll put you safely on the ground." Set your child down. Play again!

Cuddles says, "Let's play tag!"

Wrong Way

When your child starts to disobey, mention how Jonah went the wrong way but then decided to do the right thing. Have your child turn in a circle and pray a simple prayer, promising to do the right thing for God.

Let's Talk

• What are some things you pray about?
• What can you do if you've done the wrong thing?

Pockets says, "It's time to pray!"

Dear God, please help us even when we get ourselves into trouble. In Jesus' name, amen.

and he sent Jesus to save us from our sin.

Jonah

"Pretend to march to Nineveh!"

Then the LORD spoke to Jonah a second time: ²"Get up and go to the great city of Nineveh, and deliver the message I have given you."

³This time Jonah obeyed the LORD's command and went to Nineveh, a city so large that it took three days to see it all. ⁴On the day Jonah entered the city, he shouted to the crowds: "Forty days from now Nineveh

Goes to Nineveh

Jonah 3

will be destroyed!" [5] The people of Nineveh believed God's message, and from the greatest to the least, they declared a fast and put on burlap to show their sorrow.

"Burlap is a really rough material. Pretend you're wearing scratchy burlap."

¹⁰When God saw what they had done and how they had put a stop to their evil ways, he changed his mind and did not carry out the destruction he had threatened.

THE
Jesus
CONNECTION God forgave the

Pockets says, "It's time to pray!"

Dear God, sometimes we do wrong things and disobey you. Please forgive us and help us learn to stop doing wrong things. In Jesus' name, amen.

Let's Talk

- Tell about a time someone forgave you.
- What's something that would be really hard for you to forgive?

Scratchy Dress-Up

Cuddles says, "Let's dress up!"

Have each person in your family dress in something uncomfortable (for example, something too small, too big, or too warm). Talk about what the people in Nineveh did to show they were sorry and about what you can do when you're sorry about something.

Announcement!

Send your child to tell other family members when you have an announcement, such as when it's time for dinner or time to go somewhere. Talk about the message Jonah delivered and how God forgave the people of Nineveh when they listened to Jonah's message and stopped doing bad things.

people of Nineveh and kept their city safe. And because of Jesus, God will forgive us, too!

207

An Angel

Luke 1:26-38

I n the sixth month of Elizabeth's pregnancy, God sent the angel Gabriel to Nazareth, a village in Galilee, ²⁷to a virgin named Mary. She was engaged to be married to a man named Joseph, a descendant of King David. ²⁸Gabriel appeared to her and said, "Greetings, favored woman! The Lord is with you!"

²⁹Confused and disturbed, Mary tried to

"Pretend you're an angel and say, 'Greetings!'"

Appears to Mary

think what the angel could mean. [30]"Don't be afraid, Mary," the angel told her, "for you have found favor with God! [31]You will conceive and give birth to a son, and you will name him Jesus. [32]He will be very great and will be called the

"The angel said Baby Jesus would grow up to be a king. Crawl like a baby, then squat down and slowly grow taller. Finally, sit like a king on a throne."

Son of the Most High. The Lord God will give him the throne of his ancestor David. ³³And he will reign over Israel forever; his Kingdom will never end!"

³⁴Mary asked the angel, "But how can this happen? I am a virgin."

³⁵The angel replied, "The Holy Spirit will come upon you, and the power of the Most High will overshadow you. So the baby to be born will be holy, and he will be called the Son of God. ³⁶What's more, your relative Elizabeth has become pregnant in her old age! People used to say she was barren, but she has conceived a son and is now in her sixth month. ³⁷For nothing is impossible with God."

"Name something that seems like it would be impossible. Then say, 'But God could do that!'"

³⁸Mary responded, "I am the Lord's servant. May everything you have said about me come true." And then the angel left her.

THE
Jesus
CONNECTION   God chose Mary to be Jesus

Dear God, you did something impossible for Mary. Help us to believe that Jesus is your own Son and that you sent him to be our King. In Jesus' name, amen.

Let's Talk

- What's something amazing you've seen?
- What do you want God to do that seems impossible?

Pockets says, "It's time to pray!"

Yes. I Can!

Be on guard for the word *can't* in your family this week. Whenever someone hears a family member say the word, the two should shout out together, "God can!"

That's Impossible!

Give your child a glass of water, and tell your child to build a tower using only the water in the glass. It's impossible! Then help your child pour the water into an ice cube tray. When the water has frozen, pop out the cubes and have your child build the water tower. God can do even more impossible things than that!

Cuddles says, "Let's build!"

mommy. God sent his Son, Jesus, to earth so Jesus could die, come back to life, and be our King forever!

213

An Angel Appears

Matthew 1:18-24

"Hold up two fingers next to each other to be Mary and Joseph."

This is how Jesus the Messiah was born. His mother, Mary, was engaged to be married to Joseph. But before the marriage took place, while she was still a virgin, she became pregnant through the power of the Holy Spirit. [19] Joseph, her fiancé, was a good man and did not want to disgrace her publicly, so he decided to break the engagement quietly.

"Joseph was going to break up with Mary. Pull your two fingers apart."

[20] As he considered this, an angel of the Lord appeared to him in a dream. "Joseph, son of David," the angel said, "do not be afraid to take Mary as your wife. For the child within her was

214

conceived by the Holy Spirit. ²¹And she will have a son, and you are to name him Jesus, for he will save his people from their sins."

²²All of this occurred to fulfill the Lord's message through his prophet:

²³ "Look! The virgin will conceive a child!

"Jesus saved us on the cross. Make a cross with your fingers."

"Put your hand on your heart to remind you that God is with you."

"Joseph married Mary! Put your two fingers together."

She will give birth to a son,

and they will call him Immanuel,

which means 'God is with us.'"

²⁴When Joseph woke up, he did as the angel of the Lord commanded and took Mary as his wife.

Pockets says, "It's time to pray!"

Dear God, just like Joseph, we want to trust you even when we don't understand what's going on. Help us to do the things you want us to do. In Jesus' name, amen.

Let's Talk

- Tell about a rule that is hard to follow.
- What are some ways you know the right thing to do?

THE Jesus CONNECTION

216

I'll Obey Night and Day

Remind your child that Joseph did what God told him. As you help your child get ready for bed, talk about the ways your child obeyed that day. When your child wakes up, have your child name ways he or she will obey during the day.

Cuddles says, "Let's obey!"

God Says

Play a game of God Says (similar to Simon Says). List things that God would want you to do, such as "Tell someone, 'Jesus loves you!'" or "Shout, 'God is great!'" and begin each of those tasks with, "God says . . ." List silly tasks such as "Hop on one foot" or "Spin around in a circle," and don't say, "God says . . ." in front of those. Talk about why it's always important to trust God and to do what he wants us to do.

Just like Joseph, Jesus grew up and obeyed God, even when it was hard.

Jesus

Luke 2:1-7

At that time the Roman emperor, Augustus, decreed that a census should be taken throughout the Roman Empire. ²(This was the first census taken when Quirinius was governor of Syria.) ³All returned to their own ancestral towns to register for this census. ⁴And because Joseph was a descendant of King David, he had to go to Bethlehem in Judea, David's ancient home. He traveled there from the village

"A census is a count of how many people live somewhere. Let's count how many people live in our house."

218

Is Born

"Walk around the room with me in different, fun ways. We'll pretend we're Mary and Joseph."

of Nazareth in Galilee. ⁵He took with him Mary, his fiancée, who was now obviously pregnant.

⁶And while they were there, the time came for her baby to be born. ⁷She gave birth to her first child, a son. She wrapped him snugly in strips of cloth and laid him in a manger, because there was no lodging available for them.

THE
Jesus
CONNECTION   Jesus came to earth

220

Pockets says, "It's time to pray!"

Dear God, thank you for sending us your Son, Jesus. In Jesus' name, amen.

Let's Talk

- What's a special gift you've received?
- Why is Jesus even better than that gift?

Song Time

Sing this song with your child to the tune of "The Farmer in the Dell," and do the motions in parentheses.

Cuddles says, "Let's sing a song!"

Jesus went to sleep, Jesus went to sleep. *(rest your head on your hands)*
Just like you and just like me, Jesus went to sleep.
Jesus learned to crawl, Jesus learned to crawl. *(crawl on the floor)*
Just like you and just like me, Jesus learned to crawl.

Baby Steps

Look together at some of your child's baby pictures. Talk about things your child learned to do as a baby and things Jesus might have done as a baby.

because he loves us!

Shepherds Hear

Luke 2:8-17

T hat night there were shepherds staying in the fields nearby, guarding their flocks of sheep. ⁹Suddenly, an angel of the Lord appeared among them, and the radiance of the Lord's glory surrounded them. They were terrified, ¹⁰but the angel reassured them. "Don't be afraid!" he said. "I bring you good news that will bring great joy to all people. ¹¹The Savior—yes, the Messiah, the Lord—has been born today in Bethlehem, the city of David! ¹²And you will recognize him

"Terrified means scared. Make a scared face."

"Turn on all the lights and say at different volumes, 'Good news! Jesus has been born!'"

222

about Baby Jesus

by this sign: You will find a baby wrapped
snugly in strips of cloth, lying in a manger."
¹³Suddenly, the angel was joined by a vast host
of others—the armies of heaven—praising God
and saying, ¹⁴"Glory to God in highest heaven,
and peace on earth to those with whom God is
pleased."

"Pretend to
hold a baby."

¹⁵When the angels had returned to heaven, the shepherds said to each other, "Let's go to Bethlehem! Let's see this thing that has happened, which the Lord has told us about." ¹⁶They hurried to the village and found Mary and Joseph. And there was the baby, lying in the manger. ¹⁷After seeing him, the shepherds told everyone what had happened and what the angel had said to them about this child.

"Run as fast as you can around the room, then come back and find Jesus in the picture."

Pockets says, "It's time to pray!"

Dear God, we want to praise you like the angels did! We praise you because you're loving, perfect, and powerful. In Jesus' name, amen.

Let's Talk

• If you saw an angel like the shepherds did, what might you do?
• What good news could you tell someone about Jesus?

THE
Jesus CONNECTION

Pass It On

See how many people your child can tell about Jesus' birth in one day. Encourage your child to continue to tell people the good news that Jesus loves them.

Cuddles says,
"Let's tell others about Jesus!"

Shepherd Fingers

With your child, hold up three fingers on one hand to be shepherds. Hold up one finger on the other hand to be an angel, and have the angel tell the shepherds something about Jesus. Then hold up all the fingers on the angel hand to show all the angels who came and praised God. Wave that hand as you praise God by telling him how great he is.

The shepherds heard about Jesus and told other people about him. We can tell people about Jesus too!

Jesus was born in Bethlehem in Judea, during the reign of King Herod. About that time some wise men from eastern lands arrived in Jerusalem, asking, ²"Where is the newborn king of the Jews? We saw his star as it rose, and we have come to worship him."

"Pretend my finger is a star. Follow it around the room."

226

Visit Jesus

Matthew 2:1-11

³King Herod was deeply disturbed when
he heard this, as was everyone in Jerusalem.
⁴He called a meeting of the leading priests and
teachers of religious law and asked, "Where is
the Messiah supposed to be born?"

227

⁵"In Bethlehem in Judea," they said, "for this is what the prophet wrote:

⁶'And you, O Bethlehem in the land of Judah, are not least among the ruling cities of Judah, for a ruler will come from you who will be the shepherd for my people Israel.'"

"Put your hands on top of your head to make a crown."

⁷Then Herod called for a private meeting with the wise men, and he learned from them the time when the star first appeared. ⁸Then he told them, "Go to Bethlehem and search

"Point to the star in all the pictures."

carefully for the child.

And when you find him, come back and tell me so that I can go and worship him, too!"

⁹After this interview the wise men went their way. And the star they had seen in the east guided them to Bethlehem. It went ahead of them and stopped over the place where the child was. ¹⁰When they saw the star, they were filled with joy!

"Count the gifts that the wise men are giving Jesus."

"Worship Jesus by telling him you love him."

[11]They entered the house and saw the child with his mother, Mary, and they bowed down and worshiped him.  Then they opened their treasure chests and gave him gifts of gold, frankincense, and myrrh.

THE Jesus CONNECTION

The wise men gave gifts to Jesus. But Jesus is a gift to us. He is the best gift!

Gift of Love

Cuddles says, "Let's buy a present!"

While you're out shopping, allow your child to select a small gift to give to someone special. Have your child take time to wrap it at home, and then give it to someone and tell about how the wise men gave gifts to Jesus.

Treasure Hunt

Play a game with your child by taking turns hiding a special object. The person who hides it will hold a hand up like a twinkling star to guide the other person to the treasure. Discuss how God sent a star to show the wise men how to find Jesus, the greatest treasure of all.

Pockets says, "It's time to pray!"

Let's Talk

- If you were one of the wise men, what gift might you bring Jesus?
- The star helped the wise men learn where to find Jesus. What's one way you can help others learn about Jesus?

Dear God, help us to look for you and the way you help us, just like the wise men searched for Jesus.

In Jesus' name, amen.

Jesus Goes to the Temple

Luke 2:21-33

Eight days later, when the baby was circumcised, he was named Jesus, the name given him by the angel even before he was conceived.

"Rock your arms like you're holding a baby."

²²Then it was time for their purification offering, as required by the law of Moses after the birth of a child; so his parents took him to Jerusalem to present him to the Lord.

²⁵At that time there was a man in Jerusalem named Simeon. He was righteous and devout and was eagerly waiting for the Messiah to come and rescue Israel. The Holy Spirit was upon him ²⁶and had revealed to him that he would not die until he had seen the Lord's Messiah. ²⁷That day the Spirit led him to the Temple. So when Mary and Joseph came to present the baby Jesus to the Lord as the

"Simeon was very old. Act like an old man leaning on a cane."

233

law required, [28]Simeon was there. He took the child in his arms and praised God, saying,

[29] "Sovereign Lord, now let your servant die in peace, as you have promised. [30] I have seen your salvation, [31] which you have prepared for all people. [32] He is a light to reveal God to the nations, and he is the glory of your people Israel!" [33]Jesus' parents were amazed at what was being said about him.

"Say two nice things about Jesus."

THE
Jesus
CONNECTION Simeon waited and waited for Jesu

Praise on the Road

Cuddles says, "Let's praise God!"

The next time you're in a car or traveling somewhere as a family, take time to praise God like Simeon did. Have each person say one thing to thank and praise God.

Action-Play Poem

Teach your child the following action play:

Jesus was a baby *(pretend to rock baby Jesus in your arms)*
Sent from heaven for all. *(point to heaven, then stretch arms out wide)*
Jesus shows who God is *(put hands around eyes)*
To people, big and small! *(stand on tip-toes stretching arms up high, then crouch down low)*

Let's Talk

• What made Jesus different from any other baby?
• What amazes you about Jesus?

Pockets says, "It's time to pray!"

Dear God, thank you for sending Jesus to earth for a while. Now he lives in heaven. But he is still here with us, too. We want to be amazed by Jesus, just like Simeon was! In Jesus' name, amen.

to come. But we don't have to wait.
Jesus is with us all the time!

Jesus as a Boy in the Temple

Luke 2:41-52

Every year Jesus' parents went to Jerusalem for the Passover festival  ⁴²When Jesus was twelve years old, they attended the festival as usual. ⁴³After the celebration was over, they started home to Nazareth, but Jesus stayed behind in Jerusalem. His parents didn't miss him at first,

"I'm going to hide one of your toys. Let's see if you can find it."

⁴⁴because they assumed he was among the other travelers. But when he didn't show up that evening, they started looking for him among their relatives and friends.

⁴⁵When they couldn't find him, they went back to Jerusalem to search for him there. ⁴⁶Three days later they finally discovered him in the Temple, sitting among the religious teachers, listening to them and asking questions. ⁴⁷All who heard him were amazed at his understanding and his answers.

"Can you think of a question you'd like to ask a teacher?"

237

⁴⁸His parents didn't know what to think. "Son," his mother said to him, "why have you done this to us? Your father and I have been frantic, searching for you everywhere." ⁴⁹"But why did you need to search?" he asked. "Didn't you know that I must be in my Father's house?" ⁵⁰But they didn't understand what he meant.

⁵¹Then he returned to Nazareth with them and was obedient to them. And his mother stored all these things in her heart.

⁵²Jesus grew in wisdom and in stature and in favor with God and all the people.

THE
Jesus
CONNECTION

Church Walk

Take a special trip to your church, or go a few minutes early for your regular worship. Let your child ask questions about your church as you walk around together.

Special Fort

Place a blanket over two chairs to build a fort. Pretend the fort is a church. Put pillows and favorite toys in the fort, and let your child crawl inside. Talk with your child about the things that make being in the fort so fun. Then talk about why you like to be at God's church.

Let's Talk

- Tell about a place you like so much that you don't want to leave.
- What makes going to church special?

Pockets says, "It's time to pray!"

Dear God, Jesus wanted to be in your house and we do too. Help us to learn from you at church. In Jesus' name, amen.

We can ask people questions about God and Jesus.

Jesus

"Shrug your shoulders like you're confused."

Then Jesus went from Galilee to the Jordan River to be baptized by John. ¹⁴But John tried to talk him out of it. "I am the one who needs to be baptized by you," he said, "so why are you coming to me?"

¹⁵But Jesus said, "It should be done, for we must carry out all that God requires." So John agreed to baptize him.

Is Baptized

Matthew 3:13-17

[16] After his baptism, as Jesus came up out of the water, the heavens were opened and he saw the Spirit of God

descending like a dove and settling on him.

¹⁷ And a voice from heaven said, "This is my dearly loved Son, who brings me great joy."

"God was very happy with Jesus. Show me what you look like when you feel happy."

"Flap your hands like a bird."

THE Jesus CONNECTION

Pockets says, "It's time to pray!"

Dear God, we want you to know how much we love you, so help us do things that make you happy. In Jesus' name, amen.

Let's Talk

- What are some ways you can make God happy?
- What are some other ways you can show your love for God?

Underwater

As your child sits in the tub, review Jesus' baptism. Tell your child that being baptized is a special way people can show that they love God. It's different from taking a bath or going swimming. Talk about baptisms in your family and at your church.

Cuddles says, "Let's take a bath!"

Great Job!

Throughout the day, catch your child following directions you give. Each time, flap your hands like a dove and say, "You are my child, and you make me happy!" Talk about ways Jesus made God happy.

We can make God happy, just as Jesus did.

Jesus Is

Matthew 4:1-11

"Make the sound of Jesus' tummy growling like he's very hungry."

Then Jesus was led by the Spirit into the wilderness to be tempted there by the devil. ²For forty days and forty nights he fasted and became very hungry. ³During that time the devil came and said to him, "If you are the Son of God, tell these stones to become loaves of bread." ⁴But Jesus told him, "No! The

244

Tempted

Scriptures say, 'People do not live by bread alone, but by every word that comes from the mouth of God.'"

"Point to the stones in the picture."

⁵Then the devil took him to the holy city, Jerusalem, to the highest point of the Temple, ⁶and said, "If you are the Son of God, jump off! For the Scriptures say, 'He will order his angels to protect you. And they will

hold you up with
their hands so you won't
even hurt your foot on a stone.'" ⁷Jesus
responded, "The Scriptures also say, 'You must
not test the LORD your God.'"

⁸Next the devil took him to the peak of a
very high mountain and showed him all the
kingdoms of the world and their glory. ⁹"I will
give it all to you," he said, "if you will kneel
down and worship me."

¹⁰"Get out of here, Satan," Jesus told him.

"Say, 'No!'"

247

"For the Scriptures say, 'You must worship the LORD your God and serve only him.'"

"Point up and say, 'Worship only God!'"

¹¹Then the devil went away, and angels came and took care of Jesus.

THE
Jesus
CONNECTION When you need to know the

248

Let's Talk

- Jesus loved the Bible—God's book. What do you love about the Bible?
- Jesus knew the Bible. What are some things you know the Bible says?

Dear God, thank you for the Bible, which has your words in it to teach us how to live. In Jesus' name, amen.

Pockets says, "It's time to pray!"

John 3:16

Remind your child that Jesus knew what the Bible said. Learning the Bible can help us make good choices. With your child, read the first part of John 3:16: "God loved the world so much that he gave his one and only Son." Talk about what the verse means as you drive places this week.

Bible Hunt

Have your child go on a picture hunt in this Bible. Ask your child to look for pictures of people doing good things. Talk about what's good about each picture and how it can help your child know the right thing to do. If your child is familiar with the passage, review how the people in the Bible story obeyed God.

Cuddles says, "Let's look for Bible pictures!"

right way to live, you can read the Bible to find out the kinds of things Jesus did!

Jesus

"Clap your hands to make loud thunder noises. Swish your arms back and forth like big waves."

T hen Jesus got into the boat and started across the lake with his disciples. 24 Suddenly, a fierce storm struck the lake, with waves breaking into the boat. But Jesus was sleeping. 25 The disciples went and woke him up, shouting, "Lord, save us! We're going to drown!"

26 Jesus responded, "Why are you afraid?

Calms a Storm

Matthew 8:23-27

You have so little faith!" Then he got up and rebuked the wind and waves, and suddenly there was a great calm.

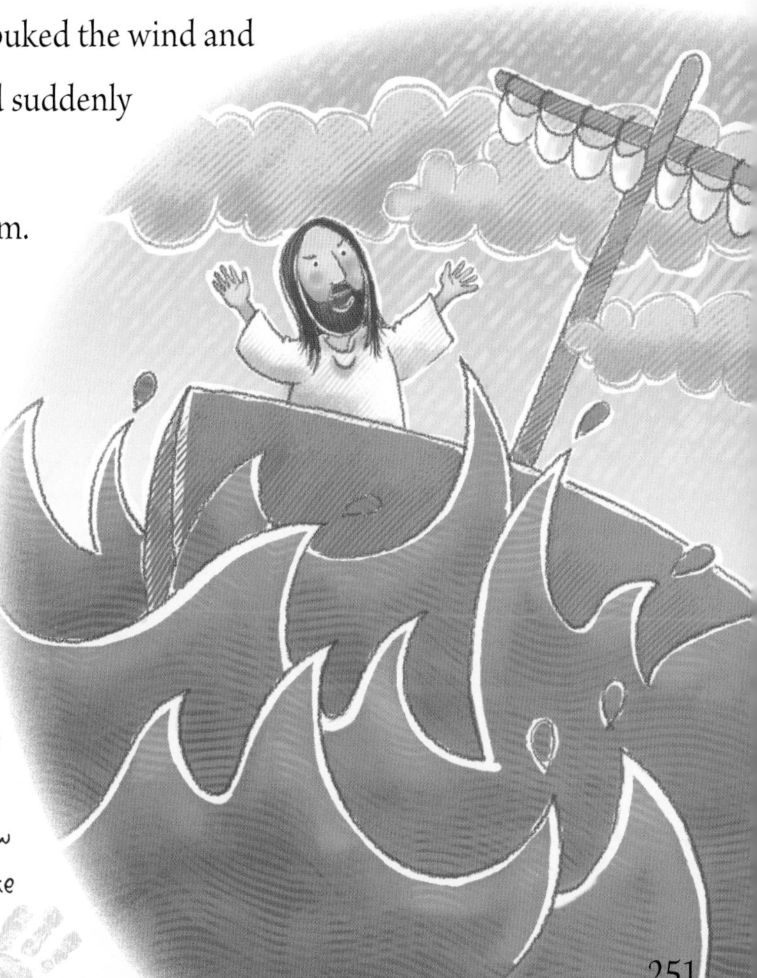

"Pretend you are one of the disciples who was afraid. How would you wake Jesus up?"

[27]The disciples were amazed. "Who is this man?" they asked. "Even the winds and waves obey him!"

THE Jesus CONNECTION Jesus stopped the storm and took

Pockets says,
"It's time to pray!"

Dear God, help us remember to ask you for help when we're afraid, just like the disciples did. Take away our fears, just like you took away the storm. In Jesus' name, amen.

Let's Talk

• What scares you?
• What's one way you want Jesus to help you when you're afraid?

Stormy Waters

Fill the bathtub with three inches of water. For more fun, add plastic toys. Have your child stir up the water, creating waves. Ask your child to stop moving the water when you say, "Jesus can stop the storm!" Watch patiently as the waters settle.

Cuddles says,
"Let's make waves!"

Raging Wind

Use couch cushions and pillows to build a boat with your child. Sit inside and rock back and forth like it's really stormy. Then stop and be totally still when you or your child shouts, "Jesus can stop the storm!"

away the disciples' fears. Jesus can take away your fears too!

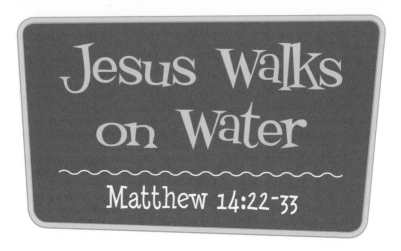

Jesus Walks on Water

Matthew 14:22-33

Immediately after this, Jesus insisted that his disciples get back into the boat and cross to the other side of the lake, while he sent the people home. ²³After sending them home, he went up into the hills by himself to pray. Night fell while he was there alone.

²⁴Meanwhile, the disciples were in trouble far away from land, for a strong wind had risen, and they were

"Rock like you're in a boat. Then blow like a strong wind. See if you can flip the page with your wind!"

fighting heavy waves.
25 About three o'clock in the
morning Jesus came toward
them, walking on the water.
26 When the disciples saw him
walking on the water, they were
terrified. In their fear, they cried out,
"It's a ghost!"

27 But Jesus spoke to them at once. "Don't be
afraid," he said. "Take courage. I am here!"

28 Then Peter called to him, "Lord, if it's
really you, tell me to come to you, walking
on the water."

"Make a scared face."

29 "Yes, come," Jesus said.
So Peter went over the side
of the boat and walked on

"Walk across the room and back to me, as if you're walking on water."

the water toward Jesus. ³⁰But when he saw the strong wind and the waves, he was terrified and began to sink. "Save me, Lord!" he shouted.

³¹Jesus immediately reached out and grabbed him. "You have so little faith," Jesus said. "Why did you doubt me?"

³²When they climbed back into the boat, the wind stopped. ³³Then the disciples worshiped him. "You really are the Son of God!" they exclaimed.

"Close your eyes. Can you feel my arm around you? Pretend it's Jesus, and remember that Jesus always holds on to you even though you can't feel him."

THE
Jesus
CONNECTION

Make Some Music

Cuddles says, "Let's sing!"

Teach your child the following song to the tune of "Mary Had a Little Lamb":

Jesus walked on stormy waves,
   stormy waves, stormy waves.
Jesus walked on stormy waves;
   we can believe in him.

Tub Time

Before bath time, help your child gather a variety of waterproof items and guess which will float and which will sink. In the tub, hand the items to your child and try them out. Then talk about how even though Jesus doesn't want us to try walking on water like he and Peter did, he can help us do other amazing things.

Let's Talk

- What would you do if you saw Jesus walking on water?
- God didn't create people to walk on water. But what is something big that Jesus can help you do?

Pockets says, "It's time to pray!"

Dear God, thank you that you can do anything. In Jesus' name, amen.

Jesus is God's Son, and he can do anything!

Jesus' Face

Matthew 17:1-9

Jesus took Peter and the two brothers, James and John, and led them up a high mountain to be alone. ²As the men watched, Jesus' appearance was transformed so that his face shone like the sun, and his clothes became as white as light.

³Suddenly, Moses and Elijah appeared and began talking with Jesus.

⁴Peter exclaimed, "Lord, it's wonderful for us to be here! If you want, I'll make three shelters as memorials—one for you, one for Moses, and one for Elijah."

"Place your hands by your face, with your fingers spread out like sunbeams."

Shines

"Point to Moses and Elijah in the picture. Now point to Jesus."

⁵But even as he spoke, a bright cloud overshadowed them, and a voice from the cloud said, "This is my dearly loved Son, who brings me great joy. Listen to him." ⁶The disciples were terrified and fell face down on the ground.

⁷Then Jesus came over and touched them. "Get up," he said. "Don't be afraid." ⁸And when

"Act like you're really scared."

they looked up, Moses and Elijah were gone, and they saw only Jesus.

⁹As they went back down the mountain, Jesus commanded them, "Don't tell anyone what you have seen until the Son of Man has been raised from the dead."

Pockets says, "It's time to pray!"

Dear God, thank you for showing us how amazing you are. In Jesus' name, amen.

Where's Moses?

Show your child the picture of Jesus talking with Elijah and Moses. Then help your child find another picture of Elijah on page 138 and the picture of Moses on page 73. Talk about how amazing it must have been for Peter, James, and John to see these men, who had lived a long time ago, talking with Jesus.

THE
Jesus CONNECTION   Someday in heaven

Shine Like Jesus

Take turns holding a flashlight under your chin to make your face glow. Talk about why you think Jesus glowed.

Let's Talk

• What's amazing about Jesus?
• What would you do if you saw Jesus glowing like a light?

Cuddles says,
"Let's shine!"

we won't need any lights because Jesus will be there!

One day some parents brought their children to Jesus so he could touch and bless them. But the disciples scolded the parents for bothering him.

[14]When Jesus saw what was happening, he was angry with his disciples. He said to them, "Let the children come to me. Don't stop

"Put your hand on your head, just like Jesus put his hand on the children's heads."

Loves Children

Mark 10:13-16

"Motion and say, 'Come on, children!'"

them! For the Kingdom of God belongs to those who are like these children. ¹⁵I tell you the truth, anyone who doesn't receive the Kingdom of God like a child will never enter it." ¹⁶Then he took the children in his arms and placed his hands on their heads and blessed them.

"Give me a big hug just like you would have given Jesus if you had been there that day. God bless you!"

THE
Jesus
CONNECTION   Jesus loved the children in the Bible—

Pockets says, "It's time to pray!"

Dear God, thank you that you love us and want us to come to you as your children. In Jesus' name, amen.

Let's Talk

- Why are you special to Jesus?
- What does Jesus do to show he loves you?

Bedtime Blessing

Cuddles says, "Let's sing!"

At bedtime, pray a short prayer for your child. Then sing together "Jesus Loves the Little Children." (You can find the song online if you're unfamiliar with the tune or words.) Talk about how much Jesus loves all children everywhere, and name some specific things he loves about your child.

Picture Card

Create a card together. Print "Jesus loves children" on the outside. On the inside, have your child draw a picture or paste a photo of himself or herself with a friend or sibling. Have your child give the card to the person whose picture is inside, and tell that person Jesus loves him or her.

and Jesus loves you!

The Rich Man Talks to Jesus

Mark 10:17-25

As Jesus was starting out on his way to Jerusalem, a man came running up to him, knelt down, and asked, "Good Teacher, what must I do to inherit eternal life?"

"Run in place, then kneel down."

18"Why do you call me good?" Jesus asked. "Only God is truly good.

19But to answer

your question,
you know the
commandments:
'You must not murder.
You must not commit
adultery. You must not
steal. You must not testify
falsely. You must not cheat
anyone. Honor your father
and mother.'"

[20]"Teacher," the man replied,
"I've obeyed all these commandments since
I was young."

[21]Looking at the man, Jesus felt genuine love
for him. "There is still one thing
you haven't done," he told
him. "Go and sell all
your possessions
and give the

"Tell me some rules you've obeyed."

267

"Pretend to hold all of your things close to you so no one else can get them."

money to the poor, and you will have treasure in heaven. Then come, follow me."

²² At this the man's face fell, and he went away sad, for he had many possessions.

²³ Jesus looked around and said to his disciples, "How hard it is for the rich to enter the Kingdom of God!" ²⁴ This amazed them. But Jesus said again, "Dear children, it is very hard to enter the Kingdom of God. ²⁵ In fact, it is easier for a camel to go through the eye of a needle than for a rich person to enter the Kingdom of God!"

"I'll hold my hands in a small circle. See how many of your toys you can fit through the circle. See if you can fit through!"

THE Jesus CONNECTION Jesus gave up his very own life so

How Many Is Enough?

Together, count how many toys are in your child's toy box or room. Then ask which toys your child doesn't play with much. As a bonus option, choose at least one gently used toy to give away to a local charity. (Note: For a young child, this may be a difficult choice. You may want to help your child choose clothing items instead.)

Eye of a Needle

Show your child a sewing needle, but don't let him or her hold it. Point out the eye of the needle, and talk about whether a camel could fit through it. Tell your child that's how hard it is to get close to God when you think your stuff is more important than he is. Talk about what makes it hard to let God be more important than anything else. Then pray for each other.

Let's Talk

- If Jesus asked you to give away something, which of your things would be hardest to give away?
- What can you do to show Jesus he's more important to you than any of your things?

Pockets says,
"It's time to pray!"

Dear God, please help us to love you more than we love our stuff. In Jesus' name, amen.

he could be our friend forever!

Jesus Heals a

Mark 10:46-52

"Cover your eyes like you can't see."

Then they reached Jericho, and as Jesus and his disciples left town, a large crowd followed him. A blind beggar named Bartimaeus (son of Timaeus) was sitting beside the road. [47] When Bartimaeus heard that Jesus of Nazareth was nearby, he began to shout, "Jesus, Son of David, have mercy on me!"

"Shout as loudly as you can for Jesus."

[48] "Be quiet!" many of the people yelled at him.

But he only shouted louder, "Son of David, have mercy on me!"

Blind Man

⁴⁹When Jesus heard him, he stopped and said, "Tell him to come here."

So they called the blind man. "Cheer up," they said. "Come on, he's calling you!" ⁵⁰Bartimaeus threw aside his coat, jumped up, and came to Jesus.

"The blind man went to Jesus. Cover your eyes while I take you across the room."

271

"Uncover your eyes. You can see! Now you can walk across the room and back without me."

⁵¹"What do you want me to do for you?" Jesus asked.

"My rabbi," the blind man said, "I want to see!"

⁵²And Jesus said to him, "Go, for your faith has healed you." Instantly the man could see, and he followed Jesus down the road.

Pockets says, "It's time to pray!"

Dear God, we know that you can do anything. Help us call the name of your Son, Jesus, whenever we need help. In Jesus' name, amen.

Shout for Jesus

When your family members are faced with challenges, encourage each other to cry out to Jesus like the blind man did. Use this fun rhyme as a reminder!

Like the blind man, we can shout!
Jesus always helps us out!

THE Jesus CONNECTION

Blind Tag

Play a game of Blind Tag. The "blind man" will keep his or her eyes closed and occasionally call out, "I can't see!" The rest of the players must respond by saying, "Come here!" They may move slowly but not run while the blind man tries to tag them. After the game, talk about what it would be like if we were really blind. Then thank Jesus for the gift of sight!

Cuddles says,
"Let's play!"

Let's Talk

- Pretend you're the blind man. What's the first thing you would do when you could see?
- If Jesus came to our town, what might you ask him to do for you?

Jesus hears us and helps us with anything we need.

Jesus Heals a Man Who Couldn't Walk

Luke 5:18-26

Some men came carrying a paralyzed man on a sleeping mat. They tried to take him inside to Jesus, [19]but they couldn't reach him because of the crowd. So they went up to the roof and took off some tiles. Then they lowered the sick man on his mat down into the crowd,

"The paralyzed man couldn't walk. Pretend you're that man. I'll pick you up and carefully lower you to the floor."

right in front of Jesus. [20] Seeing their faith, Jesus said to the man, "Young man, your sins are forgiven."

[21] But the Pharisees and teachers of religious law said to themselves, "Who does he think he is? That's blasphemy! Only God can forgive sins!"

[22] Jesus knew what they were thinking, so he asked them, "Why do you question this in your hearts? [23] Is it easier to say 'Your sins are forgiven,' or 'Stand up and walk'? [24] So I will prove to you that the Son of Man has the authority on earth to forgive sins." Then Jesus turned to the paralyzed

"The Pharisees were angry at Jesus. Make an angry face."

275

"Stand up and jump around."

man and said, "Stand up, pick up your mat, and go home!" ²⁵And immediately, as everyone watched, the man jumped up, picked up his mat, and went home praising God. ²⁶Everyone was gripped with great wonder and awe, and they praised God, exclaiming, "We have seen amazing things today!"

"Hold your hands up and say, 'God, you're amazing!'"

THE Jesus CONNECTION We can bring our friends to Jesus by

Immobile

Cuddles says, "Let's lie still!"

Have your child lie flat and try not to move. Talk about what it would be like to be paralyzed, and what it might have been like for the paralyzed man to be able to walk for the first time. Then think of other amazing things Jesus does.

Get Low

Tie a paper clip to a long piece of string. Set an empty plastic cup on the floor. Take turns standing up straight beside the cup and trying to lower the paper clip into it—like the man's friends lowered him. After each successful turn, stop and thank Jesus for something.

Let's Talk

• If there was a crowded room and Jesus was inside, how would you get to him?
• Tell about a time when Jesus helped you or someone you know get well.

Pockets says, "It's time to pray!"

Dear God, we know you can forgive our sins, and you can make us well when we're sick. We praise you for being so amazing. In Jesus' name, amen.

telling them some of our favorite stories about Jesus!

Jesus Heals

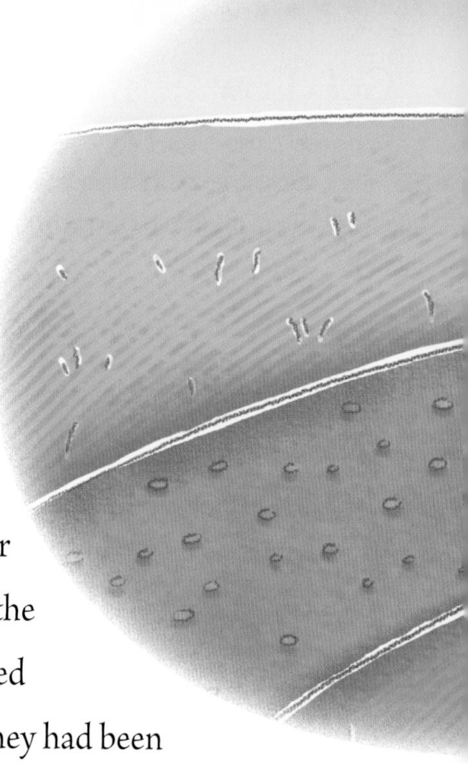

"Hold out your arms and say, 'Welcome!' to Jesus."

On the other side of the lake the crowds welcomed Jesus, because they had been waiting for him. [41] Then a man named Jairus, a leader of the local synagogue, came and fell at Jesus' feet, pleading with him to come home with him. [42] His only daughter, who was about twelve years old, was dying.

278

Jairus's Daughter

As Jesus went with him, he was surrounded by the crowds. ⁴³A woman in the crowd had suffered for twelve years with constant bleeding, and she could find no cure. ⁴⁴Coming up behind

Jesus, she touched the fringe of his robe.  Immediately, the bleeding stopped.

⁴⁹While he was still speaking to her, a messenger arrived from the home of Jairus, the leader of the synagogue. He told him,

"fringe is a stringy edge of a piece of cloth. Find a piece of cloth to touch."

"Make lou crying sound

280

"Your daughter
is dead. There's no use
troubling the Teacher now."

⁵⁰But when Jesus heard what had happened,
he said to Jairus, "Don't be afraid. Just have
faith, and she will be healed."

⁵¹When they arrived at the house, Jesus
wouldn't let anyone go in with him except
Peter, John, James, and the little girl's father
and mother. ⁵²The house was filled with people
weeping and wailing, but he said, "Stop the
weeping! She isn't dead; she's only asleep."

"Show what Jairus's
face might have
looked like
when he got
this sad news."

281

[53]But the crowd laughed at him because they all knew she had died. [54]Then Jesus took her by the hand and said in a loud voice, "My child, get up!" [55]And at that moment her life returned, and she immediately stood up!  Then Jesus told them to give her something to eat.

"Stand up really quickly."

THE
Jesus
CONNECTION

Let's Talk

- What things make you sad?
- What can you say to Jesus when you're sad and need help?

Dear God, thank you for showing us that you care about people. Remind us to ask for your help when we're sad. In Jesus' name, amen.

Pockets says, "It's time to pray!"

Get Up

This week, whenever you wake your child in the morning or from a nap, gently say, "My child, get up!" Hug your child, and then talk about how Jesus helped Jairus and his family.

First Aid

With your child, check to be sure your family's first-aid kit or medicine cabinet is up to date. Have your child count how many of each supply you have. Restock as needed. Add a picture of Jesus to remind you to pray whenever someone gets hurt, and talk about how Jesus' help is even better than a Band-Aid.

Cuddles says, "Let's be ready!"

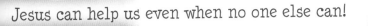

Jesus can help us even when no one else can!

The Good Samaritan

Luke 10:30-37

Jesus replied with a story: "A Jewish man was traveling from Jerusalem down to Jericho, and he was attacked by bandits. They stripped him of his clothes, beat him up, and left him half dead beside the road.

31"By chance a priest came along.

"Walk across the
room and back,
staying really
close to one wall."

But when he saw
the man lying there, he
crossed to the other side of
the road and passed him by.
³²A Temple assistant walked
over and looked at him lying
there, but he also passed by on the
other side.

³³"Then a despised Samaritan came
along, and when he saw the man, he felt
compassion for him. ³⁴Going over to him,
the Samaritan soothed his wounds with olive
oil and wine and bandaged
them. Then he put
the man on his
own donkey
and took him

"Point to a boo-
boo you have or
to a place where
you had one.'"

"Point to the coins in the picture."

to an inn, where he took care of him. ³⁵The next day he handed the innkeeper two silver coins, telling him, 'Take care of this man. If his bill runs higher than this, I'll pay you the next time I'm here.'

³⁶"Now which of these three would you say was a neighbor to the man who was attacked by bandits?" Jesus asked.

³⁷The man replied, "The one who showed him mercy."

Then Jesus said, "Yes, now go and do the same."

THE Jesus CONNECTION

Helping Hands

With your child, look for people who need help, and help those people. For example, your child might help your family clean up around the house or help someone at the store get something off the bottom shelf.

Soothing Oil

Get out some olive or vegetable oil and rub a little on your child's hand. Remind your child how the Samaritan used olive oil to help soothe the man's wounds. Talk about ways you can help other people feel better when they're sick or hurt or sad.

Let's Talk

• Tell about a time you were kind and helpful to someone.
• What's one way you can be kind and helpful today?

Pockets says, "It's time to pray!"

Dear God, we want to be kind to other people who need our help. Show us ways to be kind to people. In Jesus' name, amen.

Even if no one seems to care about us, Jesus cares.

Mary and Martha

As Jesus and the disciples continued on their way to Jerusalem, they came to a certain village where a woman named Martha welcomed him into her home. ³⁹Her sister, Mary, sat at the Lord's feet,

Visit with Jesus

Luke 10:38-42

listening to what he taught.  ⁴⁰But Martha was distracted by the big dinner she was preparing. She came to Jesus and said, "Lord, doesn't it seem unfair to you that my sister just sits here while I do all the work? Tell her to come and help me."

"Sit in front of my feet."

"Say in your best whiny voice, 'No fair!'"

⁴¹But the Lord said to her, "My dear Martha, you are worried and upset over all these details! ⁴²There is only one thing worth being concerned about. Mary has discovered it, and it will not be taken away from her."

THE
Jesus
CONNECTION Jesus wants

Pockets says, "It's time to pray!"

Dear God, help us take time to sit still and listen to Jesus' words in the Bible. In Jesus' name, amen.

Let's Talk

- What makes it hard to sit quietly?
- How can we listen to Jesus this week?

Shhh!

Spend a few minutes playing the Quiet Game with your child. See how long you can sit and listen. Then talk about what you heard, and think of ways your family can listen quietly to what Jesus might be teaching them.

Cuddles says, "Let's listen!"

Stop and Go

Play a stop-and-go game the next time your child cleans up toys. When you say, "Martha," your child will put things away busily. When you say, "Mary," your child will stop and sit down quickly. When all the toys have been put away, talk about how it's important to do things for Jesus *and* to be still and listen to him.

to spend time with us—just like he did with Mary.

The Sheep and

"Find the sheep in the picture."

Jesus told them this story: ⁴"If a man has a hundred sheep and one of them gets lost, what will he do? Won't he leave the ninety-nine others in the wilderness and go to search for the one that is lost until he finds it? ⁵And when he has found it, he will joyfully carry it home on his shoulders. ⁶When he arrives, he will call together his friends and neighbors, saying,

Coin Are Found

'Rejoice with me because I have found my lost sheep.' ⁷In the same way, there is more joy in heaven over one lost sinner who repents and returns to God than over ninety-nine others who are righteous and haven't strayed away!

"Clap your hands to show how happy you are."

"Find the coin in the picture."

"Jump up and down to show how excited you are."

"Shout a happy cheer!"

[8]"Or suppose a woman has ten silver coins and loses one. Won't she light a lamp and sweep the entire house and search carefully until she finds it? [9]And when she finds it, she will call in her friends and neighbors and say, 'Rejoice with me because I have found my lost coin.' [10]In the same way, there is joy in the presence of God's angels when even one sinner repents."

Pockets says, "It's time to pray!"

Dear God, thank you that you love us so much. Thank you that you always look for us like a shepherd looks for his sheep and like a woman looks for her lost money. In Jesus' name, amen.

Let's Talk

- Tell about a time you lost something and looked for it.
- Name all the places where God can find you.

THE
Jesus CONNECTION

Hide and Find

Hide some toys, and use a flashlight to look for them. Talk about how God knew right where those toys were and how he always knows where we are.

Cuddles says,
"Let's play!"

Counting Coins

The next time you use change, show the coins to your child. You could count them, compare how they're alike and different, and discuss what coins are used for. Talk about how the woman felt when she lost her coin and how God might feel when people try to go far away from him and forget about him.

Jesus will always look for us wherever we are!

A Son

"Hold up two fingers."

To illustrate the point further, Jesus told them this story: "A man had two sons. [12] The younger son told his father, 'I want my share of your estate now before you die.' So his father agreed to divide his wealth between his sons.

Runs Away
Luke 15:11-24

¹³"A few days later this younger son packed all his belongings and moved to a distant land, and there he wasted all his money in wild living. ¹⁴About the time his money ran out, a great famine swept over the land, and he

"Pretend to pack a suitcase."

"What does a pig say?"

began to starve.

[15] He persuaded a local farmer to hire him, and the man sent him into his fields to feed the pigs. [16] The young man became so hungry that even the pods he was feeding the pigs looked good to him. But no one gave him anything.

[20] "So he returned home to his father. And while he was still a long way off, his father

saw him
coming.
Filled with love
and compassion, he ran
to his son, embraced him, and
kissed him.  ²¹His son said to him,
'Father, I have sinned against both heaven
and you, and I am no longer worthy
of being called your son.'

²²"But his father said to the servants,
'Quick! Bring the finest robe in
the house and put it

"Go across the room. Then I'll run to you and give you a hug."

on him. Get a ring for his finger and sandals for his feet. ²³ And kill the calf we have been fattening. We must celebrate with a feast, ²⁴ for this son of mine was dead and has now returned to life. He was lost, but now he is found.' So the party began."

"Jump up and down like you're having fun at a party."

THE Jesus CONNECTION

We can come to Jesus by asking him to forgive us when we've done something wrong.

Near and Far

Have your child pretend to be the lost son. Your child will run across the room, then act hungry. When you say, "Come home!" have your child come back to you for a big hug. Talk about how you and God will always love your child, no matter what.

Cuddles says, "Let's play a pretend game!"

All Gone!

Have your child draw on a paper towel using a washable marker. Then run the paper towel under some water and show your child how the picture disappears. Talk about how God forgives us and makes the bad things we do disappear.

Pockets says, "It's time to pray!"

Let's Talk

- Tell about a time you disobeyed. God loves you even when you do wrong things!
- What does God do to show you he loves you?

Dear God, thank you that you love us like the father loved his son. Help us always come back to you by telling you how sorry we are when we've done things that are wrong. In Jesus' name, amen.

"Call to me,
pretending you
have a boo-boo
you want me to
help you with."

As Jesus continued on toward Jerusalem, he reached the border between Galilee and Samaria. ¹²As he entered a village there, ten lepers stood at a distance, ¹³crying out, "Jesus, Master, have mercy on us!"

¹⁴He looked at them and said, "Go show yourselves to the priests." And as they went, they were cleansed of their leprosy.

Heals 10 Lepers

Luke 17:11-19

"Tell Jesus
something you're
thankful for."

¹⁵One of them, when he saw that he was healed, came back to Jesus, shouting, "Praise God!" ¹⁶He fell to the ground at Jesus' feet, thanking him for what he had done.  This man was a Samaritan.

"Jesus took away the lepers' itchy sores. Scratch yourself; then stop itching and say, 'Ahh!'"

¹⁷Jesus asked, "Didn't I heal ten men? Where are the other nine? ¹⁸Has no one returned to give glory to God except this foreigner?" ¹⁹And Jesus said to the man, "Stand up and go. Your faith has healed you."

THE
Jesus
CONNECTION Jesus has made us all better—and

Pockets says,
"It's time to pray!"

Dear God, thank you for our family and for all the things you've done to help us feel better. In Jesus' name, amen.

Let's Talk

• Name some good things God has done for you.
• What can you do to show God you're thankful for the ways he helps you?

Potato Blessings

Make mashed potatoes, and let your child cover his or her clean hands in potato. Tell your child that lepers have a disease that makes their skin look funny. Scrape off the potato and talk about how Jesus healed the lepers. Then help your child wash his or her hands as you thank Jesus together for the times he has helped you get well.

Cuddles says,
"Let's eat!"

Finger Play

Help your child make finger puppets by drawing faces on 10 small pieces of paper and taping them to all 10 fingers. Re-enact the Bible passage, pretending the puppets are the 10 lepers Jesus healed, including the one who came back to say thanks.

he's forgiven us for the bad things we do.

Jesus and Zacchaeus Become Friends

Luke 19:1-10

"Zacchaeus was very short. See if you can find him in this picture."

Jesus entered Jericho and made his way through the town. ²There was a man there named Zacchaeus. He was the chief tax collector in the region, and he had become very rich. ³He tried to get a look at Jesus, but he was too

"Let's use our hands and pretend to climb up a tree, just like Zacchaeus did."

short to see over the crowd. ⁴So he ran ahead and climbed a sycamore-fig tree beside the road, for Jesus was going to pass that way.

⁵When Jesus came by, he looked up at Zacchaeus and called him by name. "Zacchaeus!" he said. "Quick, come down! I must be a guest in your home today."

⁶Zacchaeus quickly climbed down and took Jesus to his house in great excitement and joy. ⁷But the people were displeased.

"Now let's pretend to climb back down the tree."

"Zacchaeus gave half of his money away. Count out six pennies, nickels, or dimes (or another object nearby). Then take three of them away. That's half."

"He has gone to be the guest of a notorious sinner," they grumbled. [8]Meanwhile, Zacchaeus stood before the Lord and said, "I will give half my wealth to the poor, Lord, and if I have cheated people on their taxes, I will give them back four times as much!"

"Tell what you would have at a party for Jesus."

[9]Jesus responded, "Salvation has come to this home today, for this man has shown himself to be a true son of Abraham. [10]For the Son of Man came to seek and save those who are lost."

THE Jesus CONNECTION
Jesus went to Zacchaeus's house and

Special Guest

Cuddles says, "Let's eat with Jesus!"

Set an extra place at the dinner table to honor Jesus as your special guest. Talk about what it might have been like for Zacchaeus to have Jesus visit him. Tell your child that even though we can't see him, Jesus is always with us, and we can promise as Zacchaeus did that we'll be good friends with Jesus.

Tree Climbing

Find a safe tree or piece of playground equipment for your child to climb. Let your child pretend to be Zacchaeus as you pretend to be Jesus walking by. Talk about what Zacchaeus would have seen, heard, touched, and smelled.

Let's Talk

• Tell about a time Jesus helped you make a good choice.
• What can you do to show Jesus you want to be his friend?

Pockets says, "It's time to pray!"

Dear God, thank you for helping people like Zacchaeus and us. Help us to be your friends and show other people your love. In Jesus' name, amen.

became his friend. Jesus wants to be our friend too.

Jesus Feeds More

John 6:1-13

"Follow me as we walk, skip, and hop around the room!"

Jesus crossed over to the far side of the Sea of Galilee, also known as the Sea of Tiberias. ²A huge crowd kept following him wherever he went, because they saw his miraculous signs as he healed the sick. ³Then Jesus climbed a hill and sat down with his disciples around him. ⁴(It was nearly time for the Jewish Passover celebration.) ⁵Jesus soon saw a huge crowd of people coming to look

for him. Turning to Philip, he asked, "Where can we buy bread to feed all these people?" [6]He was testing Philip, for he already knew what he was going to do.

[7]Philip replied, "Even if we worked for

"Let's make a hill of pillows or blankets for us to sit on while we finish reading this part of the Bible."

311

"Shrug your shoulders like you don't know what to do."

months, we wouldn't have enough money to feed them!"

⁸Then Andrew, Simon Peter's brother, spoke up. ⁹"There's a young boy here with

five barley loaves and two
fish. But what good is that with
this huge crowd?"

¹⁰"Tell everyone to sit down," Jesus said.
So they all sat down on the grassy slopes.
(The men alone numbered about 5,000.)
¹¹Then Jesus took the loaves, gave thanks to
God, and distributed them to the people.
Afterward he did the same with the fish.

"Hold up five
fingers on one
hand and two
fingers on your
other hand."

And they all ate as much as they wanted.  ¹²After everyone was full, Jesus told his disciples, "Now gather the leftovers, so that nothing is wasted." ¹³So they picked up the pieces and filled twelve baskets with scraps left by the people who had eaten from the five barley loaves.

"Pretend to eat some bread."

"Count the baskets in the picture."

THE Jesus CONNECTION Jesus can still do

Dear God, your amazing miracles show us you can give us the food we need. Thank you for taking care of us and loving us. In Jesus' name, amen.

Let's Talk

• What do you think was special about what Jesus did?
• What are some of your favorite foods that God provides for you?

Pockets says, "It's time to pray!"

Food for All

At dinner, have each person serve one food item to the rest of the family. Talk about the miracle of Jesus' feeding more than 5,000 people with just a little bit of food, and remind your family that God takes care of all of you.

Song Time

Sing this song with your child, to the tune of "Twinkle, Twinkle, Little Star."

God takes care of you and me.
He loves all of us, you see.
"We are hungry," the crowd said.
He fed them some fish and
bread.
God takes care of you and me.
He loves all of us, you see.

Cuddles says, "Let's sing!"

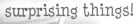
surprising things!

Jesus Is the Good Shepherd

John 10:1-15

"Pretend to open a gate and walk through it like a shepherd."

I tell you the truth, anyone who sneaks over the wall of a sheepfold, rather than going through the gate, must surely be a thief and a robber! ²But the one who enters through the gate is the shepherd of the sheep.

³The gatekeeper opens the gate for him, and the sheep recognize his voice and come to him. He calls his own sheep by name and leads them out. ⁴After he has gathered his own flock, he walks ahead of them, and they follow him because they know his voice.

"Baa like a sheep."

"Close your eyes, and follow my voice to cross the room."

317

¹⁴"I am the good shepherd; I know my own sheep, and they know me, ¹⁵just as my Father knows me and I know the Father. So I sacrifice my life for the sheep."

THE
Jesus
CONNECTION

Pockets says, "It's time to pray!"

Dear God, thank you for knowing us and taking care of us. Help us to always listen to your words in the Bible and to do what you say. In Jesus' name, amen.

Let's Talk

- A shepherd takes care of his sheep. How does Jesus take care of you?
- What special things do you think Jesus knows about you?

Take Care

With your child, look for people or animals taking care of each other. You might see an owner walking a dog or a mom holding a baby. Whenever you point out someone being caring, talk about how Jesus takes care of us.

Cuddles says, "Let's look around!"

Hide and Listen

Have your child hold a stuffed animal (a sheep if you have one). While your child covers his or her eyes and counts to ten, hide. Once you're hidden, call out, "Sheep, come follow me!" Have your child find you by following your voice. Take turns being the hider and seeker.

You are one of Jesus' sheep. Your Shepherd, Jesus, gave his life and then came back to life for *you!*

Jesus Heals Lazarus

John 11:17-44

When Jesus arrived at Bethany, he was told that Lazarus had already been in his grave for four days.

"Pretend to cry."

²¹Martha said to Jesus, "Lord, if only you had been here, my brother would not have died. ²²But even now I know that God will give you whatever you ask."

"Lie down, and then get up."

²³Jesus told her, "Your brother will rise again."

²⁴"Yes," Martha said, "he will rise when everyone else rises, at the last day."

²⁵Jesus told her, "I am the resurrection and the life. Anyone who believes in me will live, even after dying."

³⁴"Where have you put him?" he asked them.

They told him, "Lord, come and see."

³⁹"Roll the stone aside," Jesus told them.

But Martha, the dead man's sister, protested,

"Wiggle around to show that Jesus gives us life."

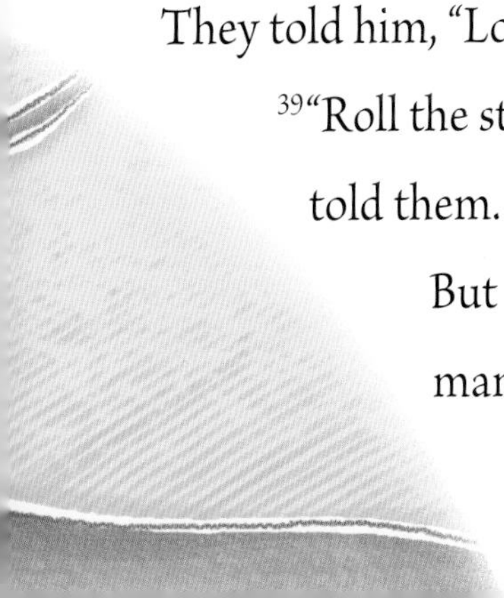

"Pretend to smell something that stinks."

"Lord, he has been dead for four days. The smell will be terrible." ⁴⁰Jesus responded, "Didn't I tell you that you would see God's glory if you believe?" ⁴¹So they rolled the stone aside. Then Jesus looked up to heaven and said, "Father, thank you for hearing me. ⁴²You always hear me, but I said it out loud for the sake of all these people standing here, so that they will believe you sent me." ⁴³Then Jesus shouted, "Lazarus, come out!" ⁴⁴And the dead man came out, his hands and feet bound in graveclothes, his face wrapped in a headcloth. Jesus told them, "Unwrap him and let him go!"

"Hop around like Lazarus coming out of his grave with his feet tied together."

THE Jesus CONNECTION When people who

Jump Up, Lazarus!

Get two blankets so you and your child can each wrap up tightly in a blanket, covering everything but your faces. Lie on the ground all wrapped up; then jump up and throw the blanket on the ground when one of you shouts, "Lazarus, come out!" Repeat several times, and then talk about how Jesus helps you when you're sad.

Sculpted Reminder

Use some modeling dough with your child and sculpt figures that you can lie down flat. Then have them stand up and walk. The figures will be a reminder that people who know Jesus will live with him forever in heaven.

Let's Talk

• What can you do to show people you care about them?
• What does Jesus do to show you he cares about you?

Pockets says, "It's time to pray!"

Dear Jesus, thank you for caring about us when bad things happen, and thank you for promising us life that will last forever. In Jesus' name, amen.

love Jesus die, he gives them life in heaven!

Jesus Rides

As Jesus and his disciples approached Jerusalem, they came to the towns of Bethphage and Bethany on the Mount of Olives. Jesus sent two of them on ahead. ²"Go into that village over there," he told them. "As soon as you enter it, you will see a young donkey tied there that

no one has ever ridden. Untie it and bring it here. 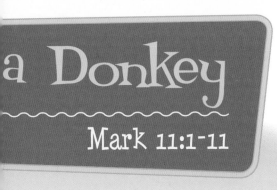 ³If anyone asks, 'What are you doing?' just say, 'The Lord needs it and will return it soon.'"

⁴The two disciples left and found the colt

"Make a donkey sound: 'Hee-haw!'"

325

standing in the street, tied outside the front door. ⁵As they were untying it, some bystanders demanded, "What are you doing, untying that colt?" ⁶They said what Jesus had told them to say, and they were permitted to take it. ⁷Then they brought the colt to Jesus and threw their garments over it, and he sat on it.

"Point to the donkeys in the picture."

"Sit on my knees and bump up and down like you're riding a donkey."

"Wave your arms and pretend they're leafy branches."

⁸Many in the crowd spread their garments on the road ahead of him, and others spread leafy branches they had cut in the fields. ⁹Jesus was in the center of the procession, and the people all around him were shouting,

"Praise God!

Blessings on the one who comes in the name of the LORD!

¹⁰Blessings on the coming Kingdom of our ancestor David!

Praise God in highest heaven!"

¹¹So Jesus came to Jerusalem and went into the Temple. After looking around carefully at everything, he left because it was late in the afternoon. Then he returned to Bethany with the twelve disciples.

THE Jesus CONNECTION

Just like people in the Bible praised Jesus, we can praise him too!

Parade Route

The next time you go somewhere in your car, pretend you're in a parade. Or have a parade by walking around your house. Wave to people as you go. Talk about what kinds of things are fun about parades and what was special about Jesus' ride on the donkey.

Cuddles says, "Let's have a parade!"

Praise Path

With your child, make a path with some clothes or leaves. Stand on the side of the path, and imagine Jesus is riding down the path on a donkey. Cheer for Jesus, and shout out nice things to praise him. Tell him how great he is. Tell him he does many good things. Tell him he helps you every day. Tell him you love him.

Pockets says, "It's time to pray!"

Let's Talk

• What are some things you love about Jesus?
• What are some ways to praise Jesus besides saying nice things to him?

Dear God, we know that Jesus is the King! Help us remember to praise and worship him every day. In Jesus' name, amen.

Jesus Washes the Disciples' Feet

John 13:1-17

Before the Passover celebration, Jesus knew that his hour had come to leave this world and return to his Father. He had loved his disciples during his ministry on earth, and now he loved them to the very end. ²It was time for supper, and the devil had already prompted Judas,

"Find the things
in the picture
that Jesus used
to wash feet."

son of Simon Iscariot, to
betray Jesus. ³Jesus knew
that the Father had given him
authority over everything and
that he had come from God
and would return to God. ⁴So he
got up from the table, took off his
robe, wrapped a towel around his waist,
⁵and poured water into a basin. Then he
began to wash the disciples' feet, drying them
with the towel he had around him.

¹²After washing their feet, he put on his robe
again and sat down and asked,
"Do you understand
what I was doing?
¹³You call me

"Pretend to wash
my feet, and
I'll pretend to
wash yours."

331

"Jesus said to follow his example. Follow my example by walking around the room the same way I do."

'Teacher' and 'Lord,' and you are right, because that's what I am. ¹⁴And since I, your Lord and Teacher, have washed your feet, you ought to wash each other's feet. ¹⁵I have given you an example to follow. Do as I have done to you. ¹⁶I tell you the truth, slaves are not greater than their master. Nor is the messenger more important than the one who sends the message. ¹⁷Now that you know these things, God will bless you for doing them."

THE Jesus CONNECTION

Jesus showed us how to be kind.

Foot Bath

At bath time, spend some extra time washing your child's feet. As you do, review Jesus' foot washing. For each foot, have your child think of one way he or she can show kindness to someone.

Cuddles says, "Let's wash!"

Follow the Kind Helper

Play a game of "Follow the Kind Helper" with your child. Do some simple chores and see how well your child can copy you. For example, you might put meat and cheese on bread to make a sandwich for someone or match up pairs of clean socks. Talk about how we can follow Jesus' example of being kind to others.

Let's Talk

• What's a way you can be kind to someone?
• What are some other ways you can be kind like Jesus?

Pockets says, "It's time to pray!"

Dear God, thank you for sending Jesus to be our example. Teach us to be kind and helpful to other people like Jesus was. In Jesus' name, amen.

and we can follow his example.

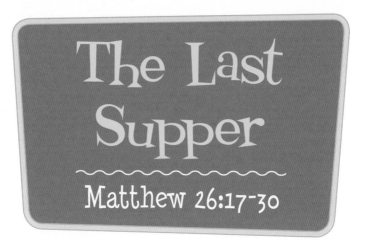

The Last Supper

Matthew 26:17-30

"The Passover was a special holiday. Tell what you eat on your favorite holiday."

O n the first day of the Festival of Unleavened Bread, the disciples came to Jesus and asked, "Where do you want us to prepare the Passover meal for you?"

18"As you go into the city," he told them, "you will see a certain man. Tell him, 'The Teacher says:

My time has
come, and I will
eat the Passover
meal with my
disciples at your
house.'" ¹⁹ So the
disciples did as Jesus
told them and prepared
the Passover meal there.

²⁶ As they were eating, Jesus took
some bread and blessed it. Then he broke it
in pieces and gave it to the
disciples, saying, "Take
this and eat it, for
this is my body."

"Pretend to take
and eat a piece
of bread from
the picture."

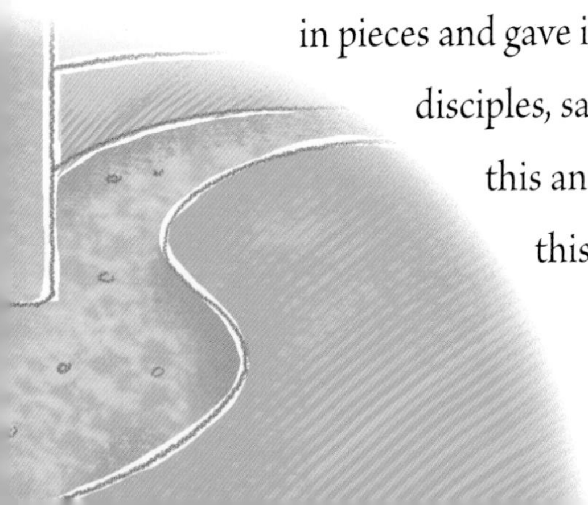

"Pretend to drink from a cup."

²⁷ And he took a cup of wine and gave thanks to God for it. He gave it to them and said, "Each of you drink from it, ²⁸ for this is my blood, which confirms the covenant between God and his people. It is poured out as a sacrifice to forgive the sins of many. ²⁹ Mark my words—I will not drink wine again until the day I drink it new with you in my Father's Kingdom."

"What's one of your favorite songs about Jesus that we can sing together?"

³⁰ Then they sang a hymn and went out to the Mount of Olives.

THE Jesus CONNECTION The Passover meal was a reminder of

A Special Dinner

Make a meal or a part of a meal that you normally eat on a special holiday. Talk about how special meals, like the Passover meal in today's Bible story, are a way to remember Jesus and all he's done for us. Jesus wanted his friends to remember that he would always be with them and that he was giving his life so that someday they could live with him forever.

Jesus Reminders

With your child, pick something that reminds you of Jesus' love, such as a cross shape or the color red. Throughout the day when either of you see that shape, object, or color, say, "Jesus loves us!"

Let's Talk

• What are some things that remind you that Jesus loves you?
• What's something you can do to thank Jesus for loving you?

Pockets says, "It's time to pray!"

Dear God, thank you for the last meal Jesus ate with his disciples. It's a reminder to us that he died on the cross the next day to show his love for us. Then he came to life again! Thank you. In Jesus' name, amen.

how God saved his people from being slaves in Egypt. And Jesus saves *us* from sin!

Jesus Prays in

Mark 14:32-42

They went to the olive grove called Gethsemane, and Jesus said, "Sit here while I go and pray." ³³He took Peter, James, and John with him, and he became deeply troubled and distressed. ³⁴He told them, "My soul is crushed with grief to the point of death. Stay here and keep watch with me."

"Jesus was sad, so he prayed. Can you make a sad face?"

³⁵He went on a little farther and fell to the ground. He prayed that, if it were possible, the awful hour awaiting him might pass him by. ³⁶"Abba, Father," he cried out, "everything

is possible for you. Please take this cup of suffering away from me. Yet I want your will to be done, not mine."

37 Then he returned and found the disciples asleep.  He said to Peter,

340

"Simon, are you
asleep? Couldn't you
watch with me even one hour?
³⁸Keep watch and pray, so that you will not give
in to temptation. For the spirit is willing, but
the body is weak."

³⁹Then Jesus left them again and prayed the
same prayer as before. ⁴⁰When he returned
to them again, he found them sleeping, for they
couldn't keep their eyes open. And they didn't
know what to say.

"Fold your hands
like you're
praying."

[41]When he returned to them the third time, he said, "Go ahead and sleep. Have your rest. But no—the time has come. The Son of Man is betrayed into the hands of sinners. [42]Up, let's be going. Look, my betrayer is here!"

THE
Jesus
CONNECTION Just like Jesus,

Dear God, thank you for teaching us how important prayer is. Please help us to pray like Jesus did, asking that what you want will be done. In Jesus' name, amen.

Let's Talk

- What things do you think are important to pray for?
- What can make praying hard?

Pockets says, "It's time to pray!"

God's Will

In the morning, have your child think of one thing he or she is going to do that day. Pray that your child will do what God wants during the activity. Talk about how Jesus was willing to do something really hard when God wanted him to.

Prayer Walk

Remind your child that Jesus walked with his disciples before he prayed. Go on a walk with your child, and pray while you walk.

Cuddles says, "Let's walk!"

we can say yes to whatever God wants us to do.

Jesus Dies

"March around the room like a soldier."

The soldiers took Jesus into the courtyard of the governor's headquarters (called the Praetorium) and called out the entire regiment. ¹⁷They dressed him in a purple robe, and they wove thorn branches into a crown and put it on his head. ¹⁸Then they

saluted him and taunted, "Hail! King of the Jews!" [19] And they struck him on the head with a reed stick, spit on him, and dropped to their knees in mock worship. [20] When they were finally tired of mocking him, they took off the

"Wrap a blanket around your favorite doll or action figure. You love your doll or action figure, but the soldiers didn't love Jesus. They were making fun of him."

purple robe and put his own clothes on him again.  Then they led him away to be crucified.

³³ At noon, darkness fell across the whole land until three o'clock. ³⁴ Then at three o'clock Jesus called out with a loud voice, *"Eloi, Eloi, lema sabachthani?"* which means "My God, my God, why have you abandoned me?"

³⁵ Some of the bystanders misunderstood

"Take the blanket off your doll or action figure."

and thought he was calling for the prophet Elijah. ³⁶One of them ran and filled a sponge with sour wine, holding it up to him on a reed stick so he could drink. "Wait!" he said. "Let's see whether Elijah comes to take him down!"

³⁷Then Jesus uttered another loud cry and breathed his last. ³⁸And the curtain in the sanctuary of the Temple was torn in two, from top to bottom.

"Stretch your arms out. That's how Jesus' arms were stretched on the cross."

"Grab a tissue and tear it in half."

[39]When the Roman officer who stood facing him saw how he had died, he exclaimed, "This man truly was the Son of God!"

THE Jesus CONNECTION

No one made Jesus die on the cross—he did it because he loves us!

Forgiven

Take a piece of paper and rip it in half. Print "God" on one half and your child's name on the other half. Say, "When we do bad things called sins, God is sad. And he seems far away." Hold the two pieces of paper far apart. Say, "We can't do anything to get close to God. But when Jesus died on the cross, he forgave us so we can be close to God again!" Have your child make a cross shape out of modeling dough or colored tape and use it to stick the pieces of paper back together.

Cuddles says, "Let's thank Jesus!"

On the Cross

Stretch out your arms and repeat this rhyme whenever you think of Jesus.

**Jesus stretched his arms and died.
Jesus' love is oh, so wide!**

Pockets says, "It's time to pray!"

Let's Talk

• What makes you the most sad about what happened to Jesus?
• What do you want to say to Jesus for dying on the cross?

Dear God, thank you for sending Jesus to show us how much you love us. We're sorry he had to die on the cross for our sins, but we thank you for that gift! In Jesus' name, amen.

Jesus Comes Back to Life

Luke 24:1-12

"Cup your hands together, then open them to show the palms. Your hands are empty, just like Jesus' tomb!"

But very early on Sunday morning the women went to the tomb, taking the spices they had prepared. ²They found that the stone had been rolled away from the entrance. ³So they went in, but they didn't find the body of the Lord Jesus. ⁴As they stood there puzzled, two men

"Dazzling means really, really bright. Show me what you would do if you saw a really, really bright light."

suddenly appeared to them, clothed in dazzling robes.

⁵The women were terrified and bowed with their faces to the ground. Then the men asked, "Why are you looking among the dead for someone who is alive? ⁶He isn't here! He is risen from the dead! Remember what he told you back in Galilee, ⁷that the Son of Man must be betrayed into the hands of sinful men and be crucified, and that he would rise again on the third day." ⁸Then they remembered that he had said this.

"Crouch down and look at the floor."

351

"Run in place and say, 'Jesus is alive!'"

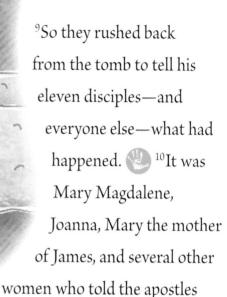

⁹So they rushed back from the tomb to tell his eleven disciples—and everyone else—what had happened. ¹⁰It was Mary Magdalene, Joanna, Mary the mother of James, and several other women who told the apostles what had happened. ¹¹But the story sounded like nonsense to the men, so they didn't believe it. ¹²However, Peter jumped up and ran to the tomb to look. Stooping, he peered in and saw the empty linen wrappings; then he went home again, wondering what had happened.

"Point to the things you see in the tomb with Peter."

THE Jesus CONNECTION Jesus' tomb was empty

Alive

Throughout the day, look for things that are alive. Talk with your child about how you can tell those things are alive, and then talk about how you know Jesus is alive.

All Gone!

Heat an empty frying pan on medium heat. Hold your child up so he or she can see inside the pan. Sprinkle a few drops of water into the pan and watch as the water disappears! Talk with your child about what it would have been like to find that Jesus' body had disappeared from the tomb.

Let's Talk

• Pretend you found Jesus' tomb empty. What would you do?
• What can Jesus do because he is alive today?

Pockets says,
"It's time to pray!"

Dear God, thank you that Jesus didn't stay in the tomb. Thank you that he came back to life and that he's alive and with us today! In Jesus' name, amen.

because he didn't stay there. He's alive, and he's here with us today!

Thomas Doubts

"Show me a scar or hurt place you have."

Sunday evening the disciples were meeting behind locked doors because they were afraid of the Jewish leaders. Suddenly, Jesus was standing there among them! "Peace be with you," he said. ²⁰ As he spoke, he showed them the wounds in his hands and his side.

Jesus

They were filled with joy when they saw the Lord! [21] Again he said, "Peace be with you. As the Father has sent me, so I am sending you."

"Breathe a deep breath in and out."

²²Then he breathed on them and said, "Receive the Holy Spirit."

²⁴One of the twelve disciples, Thomas (nicknamed the Twin), was not with the others when Jesus came. ²⁵They told him, "We have seen the Lord!"

But he replied, "I won't believe it unless I see the nail wounds in his hands, put my fingers into them, and place my hand into the wound in his side."

²⁶Eight days later the disciples were together again, and this time Thomas was with them. The doors were locked; but suddenly, as before, Jesus was standing among them. "Peace be with you," he said. ²⁷Then he said to Thomas, "Put your finger here, and look at my hands.

"Touch the inside of your wrist and tell what you think Jesus' hands felt like."

357

Put your hand into the wound in my side. Don't be faithless any longer. Believe!"

[28]"My Lord and my God!" Thomas exclaimed.

[29]Then Jesus told him, "You believe because you have seen me. Blessed are those who believe without seeing me."

"Cover your eyes and thank Jesus for being alive."

THE
Jesus
CONNECTION

Let's Talk

- How do you think Jesus got into the locked room?
- Name some times when Jesus is with you.

Pockets says, "It's time to pray!"

I Believe!

With your child, make a list of things you can't see, but you believe in. Examples include wind, love, happiness, and someone you love who is far away. Draw pictures to represent those things, such as wind blowing a person's hair, two people hugging, a happy face, and the face of a person you love who is far away. Talk about how you know those things or people are real even though you can't see them. Then talk about how you know Jesus is real.

Believing without Seeing

The next time you're in your car, have your child close his or her eyes while you describe what you're passing. If there are other passengers, take turns so your child can describe the scenery. Talk about what makes it easy or hard to believe when you can't see. Then talk about how you believe in Jesus even though you can't see him. (If your child won't keep his or her eyes closed, use that as a teachable moment. Talk about how hard it is to believe what's outside without looking.)

Cuddles says, "Let's drive!"

We can't see Jesus—but we believe in him!

Jesus and the Miraculous Catch of Fish

John 21:3-11

"Pretend to cast a fishing net, and see if you can catch anything."

Simon Peter said, "I'm going fishing."

"We'll come, too," they all said. So they went out in the boat, but they caught nothing all night.

⁴ At dawn Jesus was standing on the beach, but

the disciples couldn't
see who he was. ⁵He
called out, "Fellows, have
you caught any fish?"

"No," they replied.

⁶Then he said, "Throw out
your net on the right-hand side
of the boat, and you'll get some!" So
they did, and they couldn't haul in the net
because there were so many fish in it.

⁷Then the disciple Jesus loved said to Peter,
"It's the Lord!" When Simon Peter heard
that it was the Lord, he put on his
tunic (for he had stripped for
work), jumped into the water,

"Cast your net
on the other
side of you, and
pretend it's really
heavy to lift up."

361

"Pretend to swim."

and headed to shore. [8]The others stayed with the boat and pulled the loaded net to the shore, for they were only about a hundred yards from shore. [9]When they got there, they found breakfast waiting for them—fish cooking over a charcoal fire, and some bread.

[10]"Bring some of the fish you've just caught," Jesus said. [11]So Simon Peter went aboard and dragged the net to the shore. There were 153 large fish, and yet the net hadn't torn.

"Count the fish in the picture."

THE
Jesus
CONNECTION Jesus helped the disciples

Where's the Food?

At a meal this week, hold out an empty plate. Let each person tell how he or she would feel if that's all he or she had received for dinner. Then serve the meal. As you eat, talk about how sad the disciples must have been when they didn't have any fish to fix for their meal and how Jesus helped them.

Cuddles says, "Let's eat!"

Fishing for Cereal

Pour out some dry cereal on one side of a clean table. Give your child a bucket and have your child try to scoop up as much cereal as he or she can—from the side with no cereal. Talk about how hard it is. Then have your child move to the other side of the table to scoop up the cereal. Congratulate your child and talk about ways Jesus helps us.

Let's Talk

• Name some things Jesus helps your parents give you.
• What can you say to Jesus when you need something?

Pockets says, "It's time to pray!"

Dear God, thank you for giving us food to eat. In Jesus' name, amen.

when they were hungry. Jesus helps us, too!

Jesus Goes

Acts 1:6-11

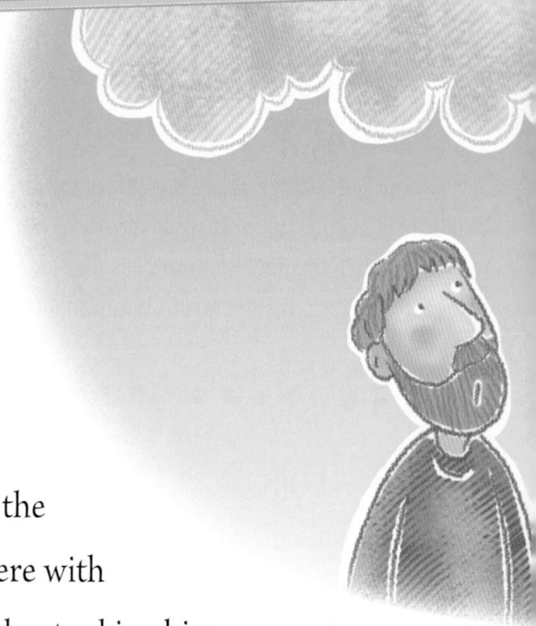

When the
apostles were with
Jesus, they kept asking him,
"Lord, has the time come for you to free
Israel and restore our kingdom?"

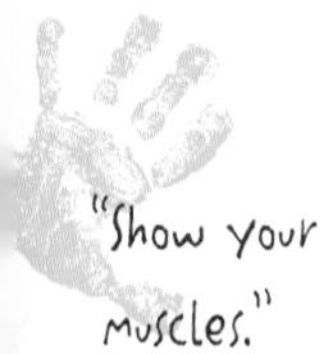
"Show your
muscles."

7He replied, "The Father alone has the
authority to set those dates and times, and
they are not for you to know. 8But you will
receive power when the Holy Spirit comes
upon you. And you will be my witnesses,

telling people about me everywhere—in Jerusalem, throughout Judea, in Samaria, and to the ends of the earth."

⁹After saying this, he was taken up into a cloud while they were watching, and they could

"Name a place you can go to tell someone about Jesus."

no longer see him.  [10] As they strained to see him rising into heaven, two white-robed men suddenly stood among them. [11] "Men of Galilee," they said, "why are you standing here staring into heaven? Jesus has been taken from you into heaven, but someday he will return from heaven in the same way you saw him go!"

"Look up as if you're looking for Jesus."

Pockets says, "It's time to pray!"

Dear God, thank you that the Holy Spirit is ready to help me tell my friends about Jesus. In Jesus' name, amen.

He's Coming Back!

When you're outside, look up at the sky with your child. Name the things you can see in the sky. Then talk about what the sky will look like when Jesus comes back from heaven.

THE Jesus CONNECTION

Mission Map

Have your child close his or her eyes and point to a place on a globe or map. Read the name of the place, and then travel around the room as if you're going there. You can pretend to be flying in an airplane, driving a car, or rowing a boat. When you "arrive," practice telling the people there about Jesus. Play a few times.

Cuddles says, "Let's travel!"

Let's Talk

• Who can you tell about Jesus?
• What's something you can tell a person about Jesus?

When we believe in Jesus, we have the power to tell others about him too!

The

"Make loud wind noises."

On the day of Pentecost all the believers were meeting together in one place. ²Suddenly, there was a sound from heaven like the roaring of a mighty windstorm, and it filled the house where they were sitting. ³Then, what looked like flames or tongues of fire appeared and settled on each of them.  ⁴And everyone present was filled with the Holy Spirit and began speaking in other languages, as the Holy Spirit gave them this ability.

⁵At that time there were devout Jews from every nation living

"Hold your arms in the air and wiggle your fingers like they're flames of a fire."

"Say 'Cristo te ama' (KREES-tow tay AH-ma). That means 'Jesus loves you' in Spanish."

in Jerusalem. ⁶When they heard the loud noise, everyone came running, and they were bewildered to hear their own languages being spoken by the believers.

"Run around the room and cup your hand behind your ear, pretending to hear a different language."

THE
Jesus
CONNECTION Jesus, who lived on earth

Dear God, thank you for your powerful Holy Spirit. In Jesus' name, amen.

Let's Talk

- What would it be like if you suddenly knew another language?
- What amazing thing do you want to do with God's help?

Wind and Fire

Help your child cut strips of lightweight red and yellow paper. Then glue or tape the ends to a strip of cardboard. Fan the strips with a blow-dryer or electric fan to represent the mighty windstorm and flames mentioned in the story. Set the fire craft in a prominent place to remind you that God's power is with you, too.

Speak Up!

During the Bible story, you learned how to say "Jesus loves you" in Spanish. Help your child memorize that as well as some of the translations below. When your child hears someone speaking another language, encourage him or her to tell the person "Jesus loves you" in his or her language.

- Chinese: Ye Su ai ni ("yea soo eye knee")
- French: Jésus t'aime ("zheh-zoo tem")
- German: Jesus liebt dich ("yay-soos leebt deesh")

for more than 30 years, now lives in heaven, but his powerful Holy Spirit is here with us.

371

Peter and John Heal a Lame Man

Acts 3:1-10

Peter and John went to the Temple one afternoon to take part in the three o'clock prayer service. ²As they approached the Temple, a man lame from birth was being

"Being lame means you can't walk. Try to scoot across the room without using your legs."

carried in. Each day he was put beside the Temple gate, the one called the Beautiful Gate, so he could beg from the people going into the Temple. ³When he saw Peter and John about to enter, he asked them for some money.

⁴Peter and John looked at him intently, and Peter said, "Look at us!" ⁵The lame man looked at them eagerly, expecting some money. ⁶But Peter said, "I don't have any silver or gold for you. But I'll give you what I have. In the name of Jesus Christ the Nazarene, get up and walk!"

"Hold out your hands like you're begging for money."

"Touch your feet and your ankles."

"Jump up and down and praise God."

⁷Then Peter took the lame man by the right hand and helped him up. And as he did, the man's feet and ankles were instantly healed and strengthened. ⁸He jumped up, stood on his feet, and began to walk! Then, walking, leaping, and praising God, he went into the Temple with them.

⁹All the people saw him walking and heard him praising God. ¹⁰When they realized he was the lame beggar they had seen so often at the Beautiful Gate, they were absolutely astounded!

THE Jesus CONNECTION
Jesus can help us help others, just as

Praise Tag

Cuddles says, "Let's play a game!"

Play Praise Tag with your family. Choose one person to be the tagger. When the tagger tags someone, that person will praise God using the body part tagged. For example, you might dance, smile, jump, or clap. Take turns being the tagger.

Greater than Gold

The next time you buy something, show your child your change or your credit card receipt. Talk about what the lame man could have done if Peter and John had given him money instead of healing him. Discuss why Jesus is more valuable than money.

Let's Talk

- What would you miss being able to do if you couldn't walk?
- What's something you can do to show how happy you are that Jesus helps you?

Pockets says, "It's time to pray!"

Dear God, thank you for healing the lame man. Please help our family and friends who are sick. In Jesus' name, amen.

he helped Peter and John heal the lame man.

375

"Pretend to share something with me."

All the believers were united in heart and mind. And they felt that what they owned was not their own, so they shared everything they had. ³³The apostles testified powerfully to the resurrection of the Lord Jesus, and God's great blessing was upon them all. ³⁴There were no needy people among them, because those who owned land or houses would sell them ³⁵and bring the money to the apostles to give to those in need.

Christians Share

³⁶For instance, there was Joseph, the one the apostles nicknamed Barnabas (which means

"Find some things in the pictures that people are sharing."

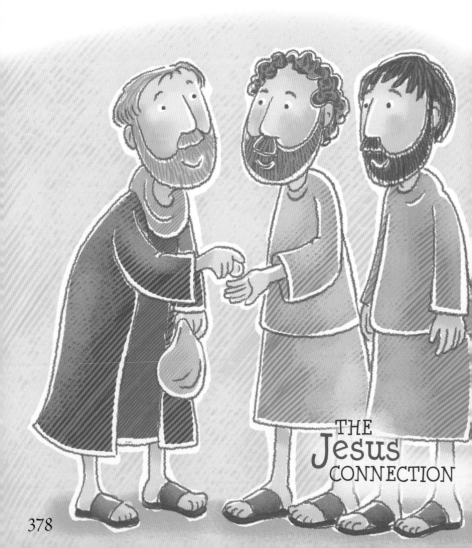

"Name something your parents own that would be worth a lot of money if they sold it."

"Son of Encouragement"). He was from the tribe of Levi and came from the island of Cyprus. ³⁷He sold a field he owned and brought the money to the apostles.

THE Jesus CONNECTION

Pockets says,
"It's time to pray!"

Dear God, you have given us so many things. Help us learn to share with each other as the Christians in the Bible did. In Jesus' name, amen.

Let's Talk

- When did you feel happy because someone shared something with you?
- What are things you could share with someone else?

Food Share

Invite another family over for dinner. Have your child help you prepare dinner as you talk about how you can share your food like the people in the Bible shared. During dinner, encourage your child to tell your guests about the Christians in the Bible.

Cuddles says,
"Let's share!"

Time to Share

Each time you see your child sharing, encourage the behavior. Tell your child you're proud that he or she is acting like the people in the Bible.

God shared with us the best gift he had—he shared Jesus!

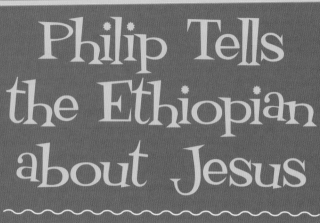

Philip Tells the Ethiopian about Jesus

Acts 8:29-39

"Let's run in place to show how Philip ran to the carriage."

The Holy Spirit said to Philip, "Go over and walk along beside the carriage."

³⁰Philip ran over and heard the man reading from the prophet Isaiah.  Philip asked, "Do you understand what you are reading?"

"How do Philip and the man in the carriage look different from each other? What's the same?"

³¹ The man replied, "How can I, unless someone instructs me?" And he urged Philip to come up into the carriage and sit with him.

³² The passage of Scripture he had been reading was this:

"He was led like a sheep to the slaughter.

And as a lamb is silent before the shearers, he did not open his mouth.

³³ He was humiliated and received no justice.

Who can speak of his descendants?

For his life was taken from the earth."

"Let's pretend to zip our mouths closed so we'll be silent."

381

"Practice saying,
'God's Son, Jesus,
loves you!'"

"Quickly find a
hiding place in
this room to show
how quickly Philip
disappeared."

³⁴The eunuch asked Philip, "Tell me, was the prophet talking about himself or someone else?" ³⁵So beginning with this same Scripture, Philip told him the Good News about Jesus.

³⁶As they rode along, they came to some water, and the eunuch said, "Look! There's some water! Why can't I be baptized?" ³⁸He ordered the carriage to stop, and they went down into the water, and Philip baptized him.

³⁹When they came up out of the water, the Spirit of the Lord snatched Philip away. The eunuch never saw him again but went on his way rejoicing.

THE Jesus CONNECTION Philip told the man from Ethiopia

Carriage Ride

Cuddles says, "Let's get in the car!"

Next time you travel in a car or on a subway, pretend it's the carriage from the Bible passage. Take turns asking questions about Jesus, and do your best to think of possible answers.

Telling about Jesus

Give your child a chance to practice telling about Jesus. Pretend you don't know anything about Jesus. Ask your child simple questions, such as, "Who is Jesus? What did he do? How do I know he loves me?" Encourage your child to tell other people about Jesus.

Let's Talk

• Name some people who have told you about Jesus. What did they tell you?
• What's your favorite part of the Bible, and who could you tell about it?

Pockets says, "It's time to pray!"

Dear God, thank you for the good news of your love that's for everyone. Please help us tell lots of people about you. In Jesus' name, amen.

about Jesus. Jesus wants us to tell others about him too.

"People like Saul wanted to use chains to tie up people who believed in Jesus! Pretend your hands and feet are chained together."

Saul was uttering threats with every breath and was eager to kill the Lord's followers. So he went to the high priest. ²He requested letters addressed to the synagogues in Damascus, asking for their cooperation in the arrest of any followers of the Way he found there. He wanted to bring them—both men and women—back to

Blinding Light

Jerusalem in chains.

³ As he was approaching
Damascus on this mission, a light from
heaven suddenly shone down around him.
⁴ He fell to the ground and heard a voice
saying to him, "Saul! Saul! Why are you
persecuting me?"

⁵ "Who are you, lord?" Saul asked.

And the voice replied, "I am Jesus, the one
you are persecuting! ⁶ Now get up and go into
the city, and you will be told what you must do."

*"Let's get right
down to the
ground like
Saul did."*

⁷The men with Saul stood speechless, for they heard the sound of someone's voice but saw no one! ⁸Saul picked himself up off the ground, but when he opened his eyes he was blind. So his companions led him by the hand to Damascus.

¹⁷Ananias went and found Saul. ¹⁸Instantly something like scales fell from Saul's eyes, and he regained his sight.

Pockets says, "It's time to pray!"

Let's Talk

- Tell about a time God helped you do the right thing.
- What's something good that God can help you do every day?

Dear God, you can change our hearts just like you changed Saul's. When we want to do something that's wrong, help us obey you and do what's right instead. In Jesus' name, amen.

THE Jesus CONNECTION

Blind Challenge

Challenge your child to do some daily activities, like brushing teeth or getting dressed, while wearing a blindfold. Talk about what it might have been like for Saul to be blind.

Cuddles says,
"Let's cover our eyes!"

Flashlight Tag

Turn off the lights and take turns hiding in the dark. The tagger will tag people by shining a flashlight on them. Talk about what it was like for Saul when the bright light shone down from heaven and about how Jesus changed Saul's heart.

Jesus changed Saul's heart when he wanted to do bad things. Jesus can change our hearts, too!

Peter's

"Hold my wrists tightly as if you're locking my hands in chains."

The night before Peter was to be placed on trial, he was asleep, fastened with two chains between two soldiers. Others stood guard at the prison gate. ⁷Suddenly, there was a bright light in the cell, and an angel of the Lord

Acts 12:6-11

"Let go of my hands and make a 'clink' sound like chains falling on the ground."

stood before Peter. The angel struck him on the side to awaken him and said, "Quick! Get up!" And the chains fell off his wrists. ⁸Then the angel told him, "Get dressed and put on your sandals." And he did. "Now put on your coat and follow me," the angel ordered.

"follow me around the room."

⁹So Peter left the cell, following the angel. But all the time he thought it was a vision. He didn't realize it was actually happening. ¹⁰They

passed the first and second guard posts and came to the iron gate leading to the city, and this opened for them all by itself. So they passed through and started walking down the street, and then the angel suddenly left him.

[11]Peter finally came to his senses. "It's really true!" he said. "The Lord has sent his angel and saved me from Herod and from what the Jewish leaders had planned to do to me!"

"Peter was excited to be free! Make an excited face."

Pockets says, "It's time to pray!"

Dear God, please keep us safe just as you kept Peter safe. In Jesus' name, amen.

Let's Talk

- The angel led Peter when he needed help. When is a time you'd like an angel to lead you?
- Where is a place you need God to help you be safe?

THE
Jesus CONNECTION

Pillow Prison

Together with your child, build a pillow prison. Use all the pillows in the house. Then play Follow the Leader out of the prison. Talk about ways God helps your family be safe.

Cuddles says,
"Let's build!"

Safe Shoes

When you help put on your child's shoes, talk about how Peter put on his shoes before he followed the angel to safety. Talk about ways God keeps you safe every day.

Just as Peter followed the angel, we can follow Jesus and the angels he sends us.

Paul and Silas

"Paul and Silas had their feet locked up! Hold your feet together and imagine what it felt like to be stuck in prison."

A mob quickly formed against Paul and Silas, and the city officials ordered them stripped and beaten with wooden rods. ²³They were severely beaten, and then they were thrown into prison. The jailer was ordered to make sure they didn't escape. ²⁴So the jailer put

them into the inner dungeon and clamped their feet in the stocks.

²⁵ Around midnight Paul and Silas were praying and singing hymns to God, and the other prisoners were listening. ²⁶ Suddenly,

"Let's sing a song to God. How about 'Jesus Loves Me'?"

there was a massive earthquake, and the prison was shaken to its foundations. All the doors immediately flew open, and the chains of every prisoner fell off!  ²⁷The jailer woke up to see the prison doors wide open. He assumed the prisoners had escaped, so he drew his sword to kill himself. ²⁸But Paul shouted to him, "Stop! Don't kill yourself! We are all here!"

²⁹The jailer called for lights and ran to the

"Earthquakes make everything shake! Shake your whole body like you're in an earthquake. Make sure to set your feet free too."

dungeon and fell down trembling before Paul and Silas. ³⁰ Then he brought them out and asked, "Sirs, what must I do to be saved?"

³¹ They replied, "Believe in the Lord Jesus and you will be saved, along with everyone in your household." ³² And they shared the word of the Lord with him and with all who lived in his household. ³³ Even at that hour of the night, the jailer cared for them and washed their wounds.

"Pretend to wash your feet where they were tied."

395

Then he and everyone in his household were immediately baptized. [34] He brought them into his house and set a meal before them, and he and his entire household rejoiced because they all believed in God.

THE Jesus CONNECTION

Paul and Silas told the prison guard that he could believe in Jesus. You can, too, and you can trust Jesus to always be with you.

Move to the Music

Paul and Silas sang and praised God even when things were hard. The next time your family is having a hard day, turn on some fun praise music, crank it up super loud, and move and wiggle to the beat in praise to God. Remember, you have reason to rejoice and be glad just like Paul and Silas. You can rejoice because God is always with you!

Cuddles says, "Let's wiggle!"

Jailbreak

Use blocks to build a prison around your child. Tell your child to sing a song to Jesus. Then call "Earthquake!" and have your child knock over the blocks to break out of the prison.

Pockets says, "It's time to pray!"

Let's Talk

• What can you do to show love to God when bad things happen?
• What are some ways God shows you he's with you?

Dear God, thank you for helping Paul and Silas trust you even while they were in jail. Help us to trust you too. In Jesus' name, amen.

<W>hen a light wind began blowing from the south, the sailors thought they could make it.  So they pulled up anchor and sailed close to the shore of Crete. ¹⁴But the weather changed abruptly, and a wind of typhoon strength (called a "northeaster") burst across the island and blew us out to sea. ¹⁵The sailors couldn't turn the ship into the wind, so they gave up and let it run before the gale.

"Blow softly like a light wind."

"Now blow hard like a strong wind as you rock back and forth!"

Shipwreck

³⁰Then the sailors tried to abandon the ship; they lowered the lifeboat as though they were going to put out anchors from the front of the ship. ³¹But Paul said to the commanding officer and the soldiers, "You will all die unless

"Lean over and pretend you're lowering a lifeboat."

the sailors stay aboard." ³²So the soldiers cut the ropes to the lifeboat and let it drift away.

³³Just as day was dawning, Paul urged everyone to eat. "You have been so worried that you haven't touched food for two weeks," he said. ³⁴"Please eat something now for your own good.

"Pretend to eat some bread."

For not a hair
of your heads
will perish." ³⁵Then
he took some bread, gave
thanks to God before them all, and
broke off a piece and ate it.  ³⁶Then everyone was encouraged and began to eat—³⁷all
276 of us who were on board.³⁸After eating, the
crew lightened the ship further by throwing
the cargo of wheat overboard.

"Pretend to throw things off a boat!"

³⁹When morning dawned, they didn't
recognize the coastline, but they saw a bay with
a beach and wondered if they could get to shore
by running the ship aground. ⁴⁰So they cut

off the anchors and left them in the sea. Then they lowered the rudders, raised the foresail, and headed toward shore. ⁴¹But they hit a shoal and ran the ship aground too soon. The bow of the ship stuck fast, while the stern was repeatedly smashed by the force of the waves and began to break apart.  ⁴⁴The others held on to planks or debris from the broken ship. So everyone escaped safely to shore.

"Pretend to steer a boat, but then crash!"

THE
Jesus
CONNECTION Jesus was with Paul

Let's Talk

- What's something that seems scary to you?
- Name one way God could help you when you feel scared.

Dear God, thank you for always being with us, even when we're scared. In Jesus' name, amen.

Pockets says, "It's time to pray!"

Stop, Drop, and Pray

If your child expresses fear this week, stop, drop what you're doing, and pray together. Ask God to help your child just as he helped Paul in a scary storm.

Ship Shape

Get a small box or disposable bowl, and allow your child to decorate it like a boat. Place the boat on a piece of blue paper or fabric. Then have your child fill the boat with small, unbreakable trinkets and re-enact the Bible story, throwing the trinkets overboard and rocking the boat. Talk about how God can get rid of our fears just as the sailors got rid of the extra things on the boat.

Cuddles says, "Let's go sailing!"

when his ship crashed; Jesus is with us when scary things happen to us, too.

A Snake

Acts 28:1-6

"Pretend to stand in front of a fire. Rub your hands together to get warm."

Once we were safe on shore, we learned that we were on the island of Malta. ²The people of the island were very kind to us. It was cold and rainy, so they built a fire on the shore to welcome us.

³As Paul gathered an armful of sticks and was laying them on the fire, a poisonous

snake, driven out by the heat, bit him on the
hand.  ⁴The people of the island saw it
hanging from his hand and said to each other,
"A murderer, no doubt! Though he escaped
the sea, justice will not permit him to live."

"Use one hand like
a mouth to 'bite'
your other hand."

405

⁵But Paul shook off the snake into the fire and was unharmed. ⁶The people waited for him to swell up or suddenly drop dead. But when they had waited a long time and saw that he wasn't harmed, they changed their minds.

"Shake your hand really hard."

Pockets says, *"It's time to pray!"*

Dear God, you took care of Paul in an amazing way, and we know you'll take care of us, too. In Jesus' name, amen.

Let's Talk

- Pretend you're with Paul and the snake just bit him. What would you do?
- Tell about an amazing way God took care of you.

THE Jesus CONNECTION

Snake Tag

Put a sock on your hand (a green or brown sock would be best) and pretend it's a snake. Play tag with your child, trying to tag your child's arm with the sock "snake." Switch roles and play a few times; then talk about how God kept Paul safe in an amazing way.

Cuddles says, "Let's play a game!"

Snake Rolls

Sculpt some snakes out of modeling dough with your child. Then squish the snakes as you talk about amazing ways God has cared for your family, just as he cared for Paul.

The snake didn't hurt Paul, and that was amazing. Jesus rose from the dead—that's even more amazing!

Life in Heaven

Revelation 21

"Tell how the city in the picture is different from any city you've seen."

Then I saw a new heaven and a new earth, for the old heaven and the old earth had disappeared. And the sea was also gone. ²And I saw the holy city, the new Jerusalem, coming down from God out of heaven like a bride beautifully dressed for her husband.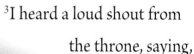

³I heard a loud shout from the throne, saying,

"Look, God's home is now among his people! He will live with them, and they will be his people. God himself will be with them. ⁴He will wipe every tear from their eyes, and there will be no more death or sorrow or crying or pain. All these things are gone forever."

¹⁰So he took me in the Spirit to a great, high mountain, and he showed me the holy city, Jerusalem, descending out of heaven from God. ¹¹It shone with the glory of God and sparkled

"You'll never be sad in heaven. Give me a big smile."

"Point to something in this room that sparkles."

like a precious stone—like jasper as clear as crystal.  ¹²The city wall was broad and high, with twelve gates guarded by twelve angels. And the names of the twelve tribes of Israel were written on the gates. ¹³There were three gates on each side—east, north, south, and west. ¹⁴The wall of the city had twelve foundation stones, and on them were written the names of the twelve apostles of the Lamb.

"Count the stones in the picture."

THE
Jesus
CONNECTION We can live with God

Heaven Song

Cuddles says,
"Let's sing!"

Use building blocks or boxes to create the holy city—Jerusalem. Then skip around the city and sing the following song to the tune of "London Bridge Is Falling Down."

**We can live with God in heaven,
God in heaven, God in heaven.
We can live with God in heaven.
Thank you, Jesus!**

Amazing!

Look for really amazing things with your child. Celebrate those things, and then say, "And heaven is even better!"

Let's Talk

- Tell me about the best place you can imagine ever going to.
- When you meet God someday, what might you say to him?

Pockets says,
"It's time to pray!"

Dear God, thank you for loving us and wanting us to be with you forever in heaven. In Jesus' name, amen.

forever in heaven if we believe in his Son, Jesus!

Jesus Wil

Revelation 22

"Find the first page of this Bible and the last page. The whole Bible is about Jesus, from the beginning to the end."

Look,
I am coming
soon! Blessed
are those who obey
the words of prophecy
written in this book."

12 "Look, I am coming soon, bringing my
reward with me to repay all people according
to their deeds. 13 I am the Alpha and the Omega,
the First and the Last, the Beginning and
the End."

Come Back

¹⁶"I, Jesus, have sent my angel to give you this message for the churches. I am both the source of David and the heir to his throne. I am the bright morning star."

¹⁷The Spirit and the bride say, "Come." Let anyone who hears this say, "Come." Let anyone

"Use your finger to trace the bright light that's all around the picture of Jesus."

who is thirsty come. Let anyone who desires drink freely from the water of life.

[20] He who is the faithful witness to all these things says, "Yes, I am coming soon!"

Amen! Come, Lord Jesus!

[21] May the grace of the Lord Jesus be with God's holy people.

Pockets says, "It's time to pray!"

Dear Jesus, thank you that you're coming soon so we can live with you forever. We're excited that we'll be able to see you! In Jesus' name, amen.

Let's Talk

- What do you think it will be like someday when we'll be with Jesus all the time?
- What excites you most about seeing Jesus?

THE JesusCONNECTION   We can't see Jesus now.

Living Water

Take a cup to bath time and help your child pour water over his or her head throughout the bath. Talk about how important water is and how wanting to be with Jesus can be just like wanting water when we're thirsty.

Cuddles says, "Let's pour water!"

I Can't Wait!

Offer your child a favorite treat, but explain that there will be a wait of about an hour. Tell your child exactly what the treat will be. When the time arrives, follow through on your promise. Talk about what it was like waiting for the treat and then getting it, and what's exciting about waiting for Jesus to come back.

but he promises that he'll come back; and people who love him—that's us—will live with him forever in heaven!